KABBALAH

Jewish Mysticism

Harry Gersh

BEHRMAN HOUSE, INC.

"Blessed is he who discerns secrets, for the mind of each is different from that of the other; just as the face of each is different from that of the other" [Berachot 58a].

It follows then that every statement made hereafter is acceptable to some students of Kabbalah, and every statement made hereafter will be challenged by some students of Kabbalah.

ISBN 0-87441-491-1

Typeset and Design by R.C.C.

Published by   BEHRMAN HOUSE, INC.
235 Watchung Avenue
West Orange, NJ 07052

Contents

Part One

KABBALAH
An Overview

What is Mysticism?

ALL RELIGION BEGINS in the unknown, in mystery. Early people looked with wonder and awe at the rising and the setting of the sun, the cycle of the moon, the changing seasons, the inconstant rain, the appearance and disappearance of food animals. They imagined that unseen beings controlled these mysteries—mysteries that controlled their lives. So they called the mysteries spirits, gods, and tried to win the favor of these unseen powers by offering them gifts and praise and worship.

Early people's attempts to control invisible forces outside human knowledge may not have been logical or effective, but they satisfied a basic human need: to reach beyond oneself to control one's destiny. Even today religion is based on faith rather than on logical proofs and as such is essentially non-rational. Mysticism magnifies and deepens this non-rational element and makes it the core of religion.

The mystical element is present in all religions, including the major western religions: Judaism, Christianity, Islam. Whether it is a major or secondary element, whether it is open or hidden behind an apparently rational theology, depends on the form of religion—but it is there. The passion of Jesus, the mystery of the Eucharist (the sacrifice of the Mass), are central mystical elements in Christianity. A Moslem Sufi text defines mysticism as an accepted way to apprehend the Divine realities, to submerge the individual consciousness in the will of God; Jewish mystical systems, known collectively as Kabbalah, have influenced the sense and practice of Judaism for two thousand years.

Most of what seemed mysterious to early people was eventually understood: the rainbow, a zebra, volcanos, madness, even the makeup of the atom have all been explained. But such enigmas as "intimate consciousness of the Divine presence," "mystery of the Eucharist," "the Divine realities," resist explanation. They are infinitely more difficult than, say, defining a new color to someone who has been blind from birth; than describing an entirely new taste. Even the Encyclopedia Brittanica (1955) begins its explanation of mysticism with a disclaimer: "A phase of thought, or rather perhaps of feeling, which from its very nature is hardly susceptible of exact definition."

Mystics, however, are not overly concerned with explanations. They seek to go beyond logic and rational mental processes. They seek paths which allow the mind to go beyond itself, ways which allow the human spirit to grasp the divine essence, to find the ultimate reality. This requires some kind of connection with that essence, some kind of communication with the Supreme Being.

God is not an object that can be seen and touched or otherwise deduced from the evidence of the senses. Mystics say that God can be known only by experiencing Him. This experience bridges the chasm between Creator and created, between Infinite and finite; by this experience the mystic becomes part of the

1

Divine Nature. (Jewish, Moslem, and Christian mystics can all live with this description, though each disagrees with some part of it.)

From the above, it is evident that neither ordinary language nor the language of scholarship is sufficient to express mysticism. Insofar as it can be comprehended by the intellect, mysticism speaks in analogies, metaphors, symbols. For example, since God is indescribable, He is either referred to by one of His attributes—Lord of the Universe, Judge of the World, the Compassionate One, etc.—or He is referred to by metaphor, a favorite one of Jewish mystics being *Eyn Sof*, "Without End."

Levi Yitschak of Bereditchev, the great master of Chasidism and Kabbalah, said: "There are those who serve God with their human intellect and those whose gaze is fixed on Nothing [i.e., God] ... He who is granted this supreme experience loses the reality of his intellect, but when he returns to the intellect from such contemplation, he finds it full of divine and inflowing splendor."

Mysticism did not appear in the western world until the beginning of the Common Era. Until then the major western cultures—the Hellenic and Hebrew cultures—were resistant to mysticism. (Rome was the dominant power, but its religion and culture were an outgrowth of Hellenism.) The logic of Greek philosophy and the naturalism of Greek pantheism were barriers to mysticism among the Hellenes. A rigid monotheism and strict observance of a religious-legal system kept mysticism at bay among the Jews.

The western world fell apart beginning in **70** C.E. when Roman armies smashed the ancient Jewish Temple in Jerusalem. Rome ruled from England to Persia, from Germany to Egypt. This was a Rome with little patience for academies of learning and the impractical ideas taught there. Greek thought became the plaything of the Roman intellectual elite. Meanwhile, a new religion spread from Palestine, Christianity, which became dominant even as it was rent by doctrinal wars.

With Judaism cut off from its center, with Greek culture engulfed by Christianity, the Mediterranean world was in flux. Imperial Rome began to crumble, and despair and weariness were the dominant mood throughout the Mediterranean world. Many found hope—or escape—in mysticism. Several mystical systems developed; they derived, variously, from Greek mysteries, Christian heresies, Eastern mythologies, and Jewish Scriptural enigmas.

STUDY QUESTIONS

1 Your participation in this study of mysticism is proof of the continuing fascination of this subject. The author explains this fascination in terms of "the unknown," "wonder and awe," and "mysteries." How would you explain your personal fascination with mysticism?

2 Mysticism did not appear in western culture until the beginning of the Common Era. What forces caused it to appear? What forces impelled its rapid development?

3 What is the end goal of mystical practice?

4 What elements of mysticism make it difficult to plumb the subject in an intellectual fashion?

5 Have you ever had a mystical or quasi-mystical experience? How would you describe the experience? Do you agree with the words of Levi Yitschak: "He who is granted this supreme experience loses the reality of his intellect, but when he returns to the intellect from such contemplation, he finds it full of divine and inflowing splendor."?

Jewish Mysticism

THE JEWS WHO SOUGHT mystical answers found them in imaginative interpretations of the texts and ideas of Rabbinic Judaism. As always, the basic text is Scripture, plus Mishnah, Talmud, Midrash. By basing their mystical speculations on writings universally accepted by Jews as being of divine source and inspiration, Jewish mystics clothed their ideas with the authority of the sacred books.

This Jewish mysticism differed in method and in major focus. Most particularly, Jewish mysticism differed from Christian and (later) Moslem mysticisms in the nature of its esoteric or secret element, in its rejection of asceticism and mortification of the flesh, and in its open acceptance of sexuality.

The esoteric element, present in all mysticisms, requires secrecy: mystical knowledge can be communicated only to a select few. Generally, the selection is by membership in an elect body or priesthood, or by inheritance, from father to son, mother to daughter. However, since all Jews are members of "a nation of priests" [Exod. 19:6], Kabbalah could not use these mechanisms of selection to keep its secrets from the masses. Kabbalists did limit transmission of divine wisdom by teaching only those persons who had reached a certain age, by restricting the number of students any master might teach, and by requiring proof of the utmost piety and ethical purity. The last was the most stringent limitation.

Asceticism and mortification of the flesh which are inherent in most mystical systems are anathema to Kabbalah. In other systems, the rejection of physical needs, desires, or pleasures, is believed to lead to high spiritual states. The denial of self, the denial of the physical body, and the obliteration of individuality help achieve communion with God. The ultimate example of Christian asceticism was Saint Simeon Stylites who removed himself from the temptations of this world by living atop a column 60 feet high for thirty years.

Mainstream Jewish mysticism rejected asceticism and accepted all God's gifts—sex included—as natural and desirable. Of course, some Jewish mystics did tend toward asceticism. They found authority for denial of the body in the commandment "to love the Lord your God, to listen to His voice, and to cleave to Him; for that is your life and the length of your days" [Deut. 30:20].

These mystics said that any desire, other than the desire to "cleave" to God, interfered with that cleaving. So they tried to eliminate all desire. Free of the physicality of desire, the soul could temporarily leave the body and ascend to a higher level.

Most Jews—including most Jewish mystics—denied these assertions. The Torah does say that we should "afflict the soul," but the reference is only to fasting, and that only on fixed days such as Yom Kippur. Moreover, fasting is not a good in itself; it is to be used only to aid concentration in prayer. Scripture and Talmud cite instances of self-mortification, but these are described as penance for grievous sin, never as proper conduct for even the most pious.

Unlike other ascetic mystics, Jewish mystics could not hide in the wilderness or seclude themselves in closed monastic communities. As Jews they had to function within the commandments of Scripture and the norms of Rabbinic Judaism, which hold that community participation and religious experience are inextricably intertwined. A Jew, mystic or not, cannot withdraw totally from the world; a Jew may not voluntarily remove himself from the wider community of Jews.

While there were communities of mystical Jews who practiced asceticism—who denied themselves the pleasures of sex and food and warmth and other pleasant things—even these communities did not see asceticism as a value in itself. The Essenes (c. 1st century) were extremely ascetic, even celibate. Yet for this small sect, whose main communities withdrew from the world to desert communes, their asceticism was a condition of a life of justice, not a principle unto itself.

Some medieval German Kabbalists dug holes through ice and immersed themselves in freezing water to mortify their flesh—but they were not following Jewish tradition; they were copying their neighbors, the Christian flagellants.

Both these examples of ascetic Jewish Kabbalists are aberrations in the history of Jewish mysticism. The great majority of mystics followed the prophets, who warned repeatedly that fasting and mortification of the body are, by themselves, not pleasing to God. Denial is justified only when used to improve man's moral actions. The prophets and sages said that acts of self-denial—celibacy, for example—contradicted human nature. And human nature is a part of Creation, of God's handiwork. Hillel went further: he said that bathing and caring for the body were a religious duty.

A statement by Rav, one of the most authoritative rabbis of the Talmud, gives the prevailing Jewish view of asceticism: "On Judgment Day a man will have to account for every permissible thing which he might have enjoyed but did not." Rabbi Isaac went further: "Are the things prohibited you in the Law not enough for you, that you want to prohibit yourself other things?"

The sexual element in Kabbalah—one could even say the erotic element—is unique in western mysticisms. The female aspect of God, the *Shechinah*, is seen as a woman with all female attributes. Rabbi Joseph, a Spanish master, had an erotic metaphor for the entire cosmos: the King and Queen in a sort of sexual embrace, their intertwined fingers forming a circle within which are the souls of the righteous. Of course, this anthropomorphic vision must be read allegorically. (See Chapter 15.)

Despite Kabbalah's usual adherence to central Jewish concepts, the majority of Jews were not drawn to mysticism. This was certainly true during the first thousand years or so of Jewish mysticism, less so since the sixteenth century. Scholars still debate the extent of the Kabbalah's influence on Judaism. In general, the attitude of normative Judaism toward mysticism is best described in this story from the Talmud:

Our Rabbis taught: Four men entered the Garden [pardes in Hebrew, used as a synonym for paradise], namely Ben Azzai, Ben Zoma, Acher [the Hebrew means "other" and refers to Elisha ben Abuyah] and Rabbi Akiba. Rabbi Akiba said to them: "When we arrive at the stone of pure marble, do not say, 'Water, water . . .'" Ben Azzai looked [thought he saw water], and died. Of him, Scripture says, "Precious in the sight of the Lord is the death of His saints" [Ps. 116:15] . . . Ben Zoma looked and became demented. Of him Scripture says: "Have you found honey? Eat so much as is sufficient for you, lest you be filled and vomit it" [Prov. 25:16]. *Acher uprooted the shoots. Akiba departed unhurt.*

"Entered the Garden" is a poetic metaphor meaning they engaged in forbidden mystical speculations. And these four, Ben Azzai, Ben Zoma, Ben Abuyah, and Akiba, of the second century C.E., were the first great Jewish mystics. They were so versed in the mysteries they were able to penetrate to the lower levels of the place above. Rashi explained what happened to Ben Azzai: The marble in paradise is so pure it is transparent, as transparent as water. But it must not be mistaken for water because, unlike water, marble is not life-sustaining.

Ben Azzai's failure was his purely intellectual approach; he tried to perceive God with his mind. But the mind, a physical entity, cannot see or feel the non-physical God. The intellect alone cannot carry the soul across the vast distance separating the physical from the spiritual. The mind can imagine God, but only the soul can experience Him. Yet Ben Azzai's desire for heaven was so great that he gave up his earthly body in order to remain in paradise.

Note

Ben Zoma's mind was not strong enough even to grasp what he was seeing. The knowledge of heaven was more than his mind could digest. So Ben Zoma's mind turned off, just as the stomach rejects a surfeit of honey. He went mad.

Ben Abuyah's mind also couldn't comprehend what he had seen. He became totally confused and when he returned to this world he became an apostate. So he was called Acher, other; that is, other than a Jew.

Only Rabbi Akiba, a completely good man, a *Baal Shem* (Master of the Name), was able to experience There and return safely to here.

The Rabbinic teaching is that delving into "what went before, what is to come, what is below, what is above," is so dan-gerous that you can lose your soul. Even such great scholars as Ben Azzai, Ben Zoma, and Ben Abuyah were unable to penetrate the mysteries without losing mind, life, belief in God. Mystical speculation is to be avoided even by those who think themselves worthy.

Despite the warning implicit in this aggadic story, Jewish mystics continued their attempts to ascend to the upper world, hoping their fate would be that of an Akiba.

STUDY QUESTIONS

1 In what ways does the practice of Jewish mysticism differ from mystical practice in other religions?

2 Why is Jewish mysticism more generally available to the great majority of Jews than Christian or Islamic mysticism is to most Christians or Muslims?

3 Read again the story of the four rabbis who "entered the Garden." Statements about Jewish mysticism and teachings given within Jewish mystic circles are often couched as allegories or metaphors. Imagination is required to "read between the lines." The author helps with an explanation of various points regarding the story. How would you explain what happened in *pardes*?

Development of Kabbalah

ALL RELIGIONS REQUIRE a "leap of faith," an acceptance of some unprovable axioms. For Jews these axioms are the existence of a transcendent, immanent, unknowable God and the divine origin of the Torah. Once one takes these "leaps" of faith, the rest of Judaism may seem quite logical—so logical that beginning with Philo Judeaus in the first century, and peaking with Maimonides in the thirteenth century, great Jewish thinkers have been able to "prove" that the Torah is rationally consistent with Aristotelian logic. There are, however, parts of Scripture that resist ordinary logic. For example, what is a rationalist to make of Scriptural passages that imply the existence of wisdom beyond human ken, outside human understanding; passages that imply the existence of wisdom as an entity in and of itself?

But wisdom—where shall it be found? And where is the place of understanding? Man does not know its price; neither is it to be found in the place of the living . . . Where is wisdom from? And where is the place of understanding? The ability to see it is hidden from the eyes of the living . . . [Job 28:12-14].

Likewise, what does a logician make of the Scriptural description of the throne of God:

*Wheel within a wheel . . . for the spirit of the living creature was within the wheels . . . Above the firmament that was over their heads was the likeness of a throne, . . . and upon the like-*ness *of the throne was a likeness as the appearance of a man . . . This was the appearance of the likeness of the glory of the Lord . . . [Ezek. 1].*

Jewish mysticism grew out of speculation on the meaning of these and other passages which could not be penetrated by ordinary reasoning. The mystics looked for other methods of penetration. Most Jewish mystics used speculative methods, imaginative musings on what was behind the literal meaning of the words, to uncover the hidden meanings.

The focus of the earliest of these speculations was Ezekiel's vision of the wheels and the chariot, from which early mysticism got the name *merkabah* [chariot] mysticism. Gradually, mystics expanded their meditations to include the many other mysteries in the whole of Scripture, with special emphasis on the creation story.

The Rabbis of the Mishnah and the Talmud rejected—and avoided—those they called "riders of the chariot." Yet despite the antagonism of the leaders of the Babylonian and Palestinian academies, early mystics produced a significant and influential body of mystical literature. The most important of the early works of mysticism were the *Hechalot* books and the *Sefer Yetsirah*.

Hechalot (Halls) described the heavenly halls or palaces through which the adept passes in his visions. The *Sefer Yetsirah*, the Book of Creation, described the Creation in terms of emanations from God and the 22 letters of the Hebrew alphabet. This introduced into Kabbalah the concept of the 10 "lights," "emanations," or *sefirot* as the bridges between the divine and earthly spheres. *Hechalot, Yetsirah,* and intellectual constructions such as the *sefirot,* were the beginning of Kabbalah.

Kabbalah, a noun derived from the Hebrew verb *kibel,* to receive, was first used to describe ideas or doctrine received from tradition. The word is used in the Talmud to refer to sacred works outside the Torah; e.g., the *Mishnah* is called a "kabbalah." The term came to refer to teachings outside the accepted texts and, eventually encompassed Jewish mysticism. Most particularly, it refers to the systems developed in the Middle Ages, from the twelfth century onward.

The Torah, or Written Law, records that it was given by God to Israel through Moses at Mt. Sinai. According to Rabbinic tradition, God also gave Moses an Oral Law, a Law that was not written but meant to be passed on by word of mouth— the *Mishnah.* The Kabbalists added another tradition: Moses received a third body of knowledge at Mount Sinai—the esoteric Torah. This is the body of secret knowledge we call Kabbalah, by which we can uncover in the Torah the secret laws of the universe.

The major process for uncovering the secret Kabbalah is speculative, called *Kabbalah iyyunit.* There is also a minor process, the practical and magical *Kabbalah maasit.* Kabbalists hold that their speculations and disciplines are not anti-rational, not illogical. They argue that since the logical mind alone cannot truly comprehend God and Creation—notions accepted by all Jews—they are merely attempting to bypass the limitations of logical inquiry.

During the first 10 centuries of the Common Era, Jewish mysticism established strong bases in Italy, Africa, and Spain. Although largely *merkabah*-type speculation based on Scripture, Mishnah, and Midrash, this mysticism assimilated important ideas from the mystical systems of the varied cultures in which Jews lived: the notions of angels and demons, transmigration of souls (*Gilgul*), the magical manipulation of numbers (*gematria*), and so on.

In Moslem Spain, Kabbalah assimilated concepts from Islamic mysticism. These the Jewish mystics, like the early Islamic mystics or Sufis, confined themselves mainly to mystical spirituality rather than to *merkabah* speculations or magic.

In a Christian environment, in northern France and Germany, Jewish mysticism took another turn. There the *Chasidei* * *Ashkenaz* ("Pious Ones of Ashkenaz") taught total repentance through absolute adherence to the Jewish laws of ethical conduct and ritual observance. Some of the *Chasidei Ashkenaz* added a Christian concept: mortification of the flesh. They supported their argument for asceticism with various esoteric and theosophical ideas, but they were actually merely imitating their Christian neighbors.

Later Kabbalah (it is inappropriate to label as modern a discipline based on medieval ideas) began with Isaac the Blind, who lived in Spain on the border of France in the thirteenth century and was widely influential in the Mediterranean area. The Kabbalah of Isaac the Blind held that among the numberless attributes of God, Divine Thought led the list; that communion with this aspect of God was possible through meditation on the "lights," the *sefirot.* The desired end of this meditation was to be absorbed into Divine Thought, and thus become part of the world above. It was Isaac the Blind who gave to Ju-

---

* These medieval *Chasidim* were not the forerunners of the very different modern *Chasidim.* There is no connection between the *Chasidei Ashkenaz* and the members of the sect founded 500 years later by the *Baal Shem Tov.*

daism the mystic's favorite metaphor for God: *Eyn Sof*, the Endless One, the Infinite.

This period of the flowering of Spanish Kabbalah was also the age of Maimonides—Maimonides the Aristotelian, Maimonides the rationalist. Inevitably, these two schools of thought—rationalist Maimonist and mystical Kabbalist—were at odds. Yet there were some Kabbalists who agreed with Maimonides and some Maimonists were also followers of the Kabbalah. For example, Abraham Abulafia (Spanish, thirteenth century) was both a passionate follower of Maimonides and a major Kabbalist. He said his work in mysticism was an extension of Maimonides' ideas, that he was simply moving beyond Maimonides' preoccupation with philosophy.

It was into this world that Moses de Leon introduced the *Zohar*, the book that became the bible of Kabbalah.

STUDY QUESTIONS

1 Read Ezekiel 1—the description of Ezekiel's vision of the chariot and throne of God. Early Jewish mysticism was based in large part on this formidable description. What is your immediate emotional response? What is your immediate intellectual response? How does contemplating this vision fit within the general definition of Jewish mysticism?

2 What is the definition of Kabbalah? How did the term come to be applied to Jewish mysticism?

3 What are the two types of Kabbalah, and what purpose does each serve?

4 What contribution did Isaac the Blind make to Kabbalah? Why did he choose to describe God in negative terms?

8

The Zohar

JUST AS MAIMONIDES' *Guide of the Perplexed* was the watershed in Jewish philosophy, so Moses de Leon's *Zohar*, unveiled about a century later, was a watershed in Jewish mysticism. Until publication of the *Zohar*, Jewish mysticism was a disorganized collection of esoterica and theosophy. After its publication in about 1290, Kabbalah became relatively structured and integrated.

According to the traditional story, Moses ben Shem Tov de Leon of Guadalajara came into possession of a manuscript written by Rabbi Simeon bar Yochai of the second century C.E. Rabbi Simeon was sentenced to death by the Romans for continuing to teach Torah after they had forbidden it. To escape death, Simeon and his son Eleazar hid in a cave for some twelve years, kept alive by the Jews of the area and by miracles. During that long imprisonment, Simeon wrote the *Zohar*. It was hidden, lost, and miraculously uncovered a thousand years later, eventually coming into de Leon's hands.

The *Zohar* is written in Aramaic, Rabbi Simeon's language, but modern scholars note aspects of the book that dispute its traditional history. For one, the author of the book shows knowledge of the Babylonian Talmud, of post-Talmudic *midrashim*, later translations of Scripture—all written long after Simeon's time. It even includes some Rashi from the eleventh century. Furthermore, the twelfth century Crusades are mentioned, as is Arab rule in Palestine (which began in the seventh century). It describes customs specific to medieval Spanish Jewry. The *Zohar*'s ideas of Satan, magic, and sorcery are also medieval rather than second century concepts. This all suggests that the *Zohar* is a late thirteenth century work combining old texts, current Spanish Kabbalist belief, and the speculations of de Leon.

A major internal clue to the date of composition of the *Zohar* is its forecast of redemption. The writer says that redemption is near because it is the end of 1,200 years of the Exile (one century for each tribe). The belief that the Exile would end in approximately the year 1300 C.E. was widespread in de Leon's time.

The *Sefer ha Zohar*, or *Book of Splendor*, took its name from Scripture: "And they that be wise shall shine as the *splendor* [brightness] of the firmament; and they that turn the many to righteousness [shall shine] as the stars, for ever and ever" [Dan. 12:3]. *Zohar* is the book of the wise who turn the many to righteousness.

The work is in several volumes; most editions include the *Tikkunei Zohar*, added by disciples of Isaac Luria of Safed, Israel, several centuries after de Leon, and the *Zohar Chadash*, texts added by later Kabbalists of Safed.

The *Zohar* is a compendium of Scriptural exegesis and stories; a map and guidebook of the mystical landscape of heaven and creation; a key by which the adept can decode the esoteric Torah. Truly, as the Baal Shem Tov said, "When

9

I open the *Zohar*, I behold the whole universe."

The main part of the work is arranged according to the weekly portions of the Torah read during worship services. This format is followed from Genesis 1 to Numbers 30 and for parts of Deuteronomy. In addition to providing *midrashim*, homilies and discussions on sections of these portions of Torah, it comments on portions of the books of Ruth, Lamentations, and Song of Songs. Like raisins in a cake, discussions and stories on esoteric subjects are sprinkled throughout. Some are short, some as long as books.

These are the major divisions of the *Zohar*:

— The *Idra Rabba* or *Great Assembly*—Simeon and his ten companions discuss the revelation of God in the form of primordial man (*Adam Kadmon*). In a kind of parallel to the Talmudic story of Akiba and *pardes*, three of the 10 companions die in ecstasy after seeing the mysteries.

— The *Idra Zuta* or *Lesser Assembly*—Another parallel: a description of Simeon's death much like that of Moses' death in the closing chapters of Deuteronomy.

— *Hechalot* or *Halls*—A discussion of the mysteries of prayer and a treatise on angels. Includes descriptions of the palaces in the Garden of Eden where souls go after death. (For those not quite ready for death, *Hechalot* says that particularly fervent and dedicated and honestly-meant prayers can lift the soul into the Halls.)

— An explanation of chiromancy (palmistry) and physiognomy by which an individual's fate can be foretold by the lineaments of the face and hands.

— A discourse on the nature of the soul derived from a mystical explanation of the laws of slavery, which is metaphorically couched in the story of a meeting of Simeon's companions and a great Kabbalist who goes about as a poor old man with a donkey.

— The mystical meaning of grace after meals told through the story of a wonder child—the son of the old man with the donkey.

—A description of the world to come which was given to Simeon and his companions by the head of a Heavenly Academy.

—An explanation of the mysteries of the *sefirot*.

—A discourse by Simeon on the secret meanings of the letters that form God's Name.

—An interpretation of the vision of the chariot in Ezekiel.

Essentially, the work is a description of and an explanation of the mysteries of the world of the *sefirot* as symbolic of the world of the divine—which reflects this world, created through the agency of the *sefirot*. It deals with the place of the Jew in both worlds.

There are many lessons in the *Zohar*, all dependent on faithful acceptance of the first three: ① There is a secret meaning in every word of Torah, in every commandment—seek it out, ② there is a supreme value in fulfilling every commandment—learn what it is, and ③ do not read the Torah literally; if you do, you will neglect the commandments.

STUDY QUESTIONS

1 What evidence do we have that the *Zohar* was actually written in medieval times, and not in the first century, as Moses de Leon claimed?

2 What are the three axiomatic lessons of the *Zohar*? Do you agree or disagree with these premises?

3 In which section of the *Zohar* would you expect to find a description of the mystical meaning of the *Shema* prayer? In which section might you find a parallel to the story of the four sages—Ben Azzai, Ben Zoma, Acher, and Akiba?

4 Read the grace after meals (you can find it in any Jewish prayer book). Which sections do you think might particularly lend themselves to mystic study? Why?

Lurianic Kabbalah

WITH THE EXPULSION of the Jews from Spain and Portugal at the end of the fifteenth century, the center of Kabbalah moved back to Palestine from western Europe. There, in the town of Safed, a new Kabbalah was grafted onto the roots of Spanish Kabbalah and the *Zohar*. This was the Lurianic Kabbalah, so named for Rabbi Isaac ben Solomon Luria. He was called *HaAri*, which means "the lion," and is also an acronym for "*Ashkenazic Rabbi Isaac*."

The *Zohar* was the first watershed in Jewish mysticism; it gave Kabbalah a system. Isaac Luria and his school of Safed Kabbalists were the second watershed. Before Safed, Kabbalah was an esoteric discipline, restricted to those already adept in it, dealing mainly with other-worldly subjects. After Safed, Kabbalah was almost a mass phenomenon. The Safed Kabbalists changed the form of Kabbalah so that ordinary Jews could reach for it and could find within it answers to contemporary questions.

The coming of the messiah, which meant the end of the Exile, was no longer a far-away promise but an imminent possibility to the Safed Kabbalists. They gave Israel a special role in the divine order, and they gave each Jew personal responsibility for a part in a God-ordered task. As a result of the changes made by Luria and his followers, notably Moses Cordovero and Chayim Vital, Kabbalah became relevant and available to the average educated Jew.

From the time the First Temple was destroyed and the Jews were taken to Babylon, exile was a constant in Jewish existence. Even though some did return to the land with Ezra and Nehemiah, they were ruled by foreign overlords. Except for the brief period of the Hasmonean kings, the returnees were subjects respectively to Persian, Egyptian, Syrian, Greek, and Roman princes. So, while they lived in the land that God had promised to them, they were in a kind of internal exile. In 70 C.E. and again in 135 C.E., they were scattered among foreign lands. Throughout these centuries, Jewish prophets and sages proclaim that exile, external and internal, was an abnormal condition. It was, they said, God's judgment on the Jews because they had not followed the commandments. The judgment appeared to be confirmed by the Crusades, the Black Death, the expulsions from this land and that.

Nothing the Jews did seemed to temper God's severe judgment. A feeling of futility became part of the Jewish condition. Kabbalah had no answer to this problem until Isaac Luria of Safed and his companions. The Lurianic Kabbalah confronted and offered answers to the Jewish sense of hopelessness.

Luria taught that the exile of the Jews was part of the divine order, not punishment for wrong-doing. Creation itself began, not with a positive act, but with a negative act: God withdrew into Himself in order to leave space for the created world (the act of *tsimtsum*). This withdrawal is, in the Lurianic sense, a form of exile. In the Lurianic system, exile is the constant condition of God, of the world, of mankind—and of the Jews.

This Lurianic system was not transmitted to us by Isaac Luria himself. While the master of the Safed Kabbalists was a man of much personal magnetism, with enormous appeal to his followers, he was neither a systematic thinker nor a writer. It was his disciples, Moses Cordovero and Chayim Vital, who gave order to his thoughts. It was they, not Luria, who actually wrote down the systematic explanations of the Lurianic Kabbalah. The absence of certain intellectual abilities did not lessen the *Ari*'s position as the Master, as pure intellect was of relatively minor importance in Safed. The Safed Kabbalists concentrated on the mystic-mythic elements of Kabbalah, rather than the philosophic elements which had fascinated the Spanish mystics. Luria developed the radical cosmic myths, and Chayim Vital and Moses Cordovero incorporated them in a theology. Luria's function was still the more important one because, as the scholar Gershom Scholem (*Kabbalah*, page 74) puts it: "A large area of [Luria's] system does not lend itself to complete intellectual penetration, and in many instances it can only be reached through personal meditation."

While the earlier esoteric Kabbalah had been the sole domain of a few scholars, the message of the Safed mystics reached more widely. Whereas original *Zohar* had been accepted as a kind of Talmud of theosophy, a sourcebook of knowledge of the divine, it had been little known, and certainly had not been read outside the restricted circle of adepts. The report of a Jewish Kabbalist, traveling several years after the appearance of the *Zohar*, confirms this. He comments that he rarely saw copies of the book, even in the homes of scholars. It wasn't until after the incorporation of the refinements and additions of the Safed school, that this Bible of Kabbalah was found wherever Jews lived.

There were three major reasons for the blossoming of Kabbalah:

First, it was welcomed because it offered hope in a seemingly hopeless situation.

Second, the art of printing had spread widely in Europe by the time the Safed school began to flourish.

Third, the restrictions on study of the Kabbalah were removed. A Safed Kabbalist explained why it was no longer necessary for the Kabbalah to remain an esoteric discipline, open only to special people:

The decree from above not to engage openly in the wisdom of Kabbalah was meant to apply only for a set time, until 1490 [C.E.]. From then on is the time of the last generation [before the Messiah]; the decree is rescinded, and permission is granted to engage in studying the Book of Zohar. From 1540 on, the best way to fulfill the divine commandment is to engage in it, young or old . . . Since this and nothing else will bring about the coming of King Messiah, do not be negligent [Quoted by Matt, Zohar, p. 11].

With this theosophical change of heart, the esoteric element in Kabbalah was drastically reduced although change would likely have come in any case because the sixteenth century was also the century in which printing spread throughout the world. As long as books were hand-written, thus rare and expensive, the knowledge in the books could be controlled. Printing made books and the knowledge they contained universally available.

Jews had been forbidden to practice most trades, but printing was a brand new craft in the fifteenth century. The first major Jewish presses were well established before princes and bishops thought to bar the new craft to Jews. Two editions of the *Zohar* were printed in 1560, one in Cremona, another in Mantua. The Kabbalah was now available to any literate Jew, as well as to interested Moslems and Christians.

The Kabbalah got its new form, new home, and greatly increased fervor as the result of one catastrophe: the expulsion of the Jews from Spain and Portugal. Three new catastrophes pushed all Jews, most particularly those of Eastern Europe, to grasp eagerly at the mystical promise inherent in Kabbalah.

In the early 1600's Shabbatai Tsevi, a Turkish Jew, claimed that he was the Messiah and was about to initiate the Messianic Age. Thousands of Jews believed him; many gave up their homes, fortunes, and careers to follow him. In 1644 Tsevi was proved a fraud, and the Jews who believed in this false messiah, who fully expected the immediate end of exile, persecution, war, and want, were thrown into despair.

Four years later, in 1648-49, Bagdan Chmielnicki and his Cossack hordes scourged the Jews of the Ukraine and Poland. It is estimated that one-quarter to one-third of all the Jews in Eastern Europe died at the hands of Chmielnicki's Cossacks. Thousands more died at the hands of those who had sworn to protect the Jews, the Polish nobility.

Betrayed by the self-proclaimed messiah, by kings, pope, and bishops, the Jews could think of no way out of their despair. Nor did they find much succor in faithful practice of the commandments. More than one hundred thousand Jews were martyred; the millions left alive had no hope. Many turned to mysticism and magic, thinking that perhaps these would bring safety and peace.

When most of the Jews in Eastern Europe became subjects of the Czar (actually, Czarina Catherine the Great) in 1793, their troubles multiplied. It was then that many Jews embraced the new-est expression of mysticism's promise: Chasidism.

STUDY QUESTIONS

1 According to the prophets and the Jewish sages, what was the reason for the exile? How did Isaac Luria of Safed explain it? In what way did his explanation lead to the popularization of Kabbalah among Jews?

2 What three reasons does the author give for the rapid spread of the *Zohar* and Kabbalah, following the period of Luria and the flowering of the sages of Safed?

3 How did the expulsion from Spain, the rise and fall of the false messiah Shabbatai Tsevi, and the partition of Poland add further impetus to the spread of Jewish mysticism?

4 According to the Safed school of Kabbalah, why was study of the *Zohar* forbidden before 1490 and urgent from 1540 on?

Chasidism

ISRAEL BEN ELIEZER or Israel of Medzibedz (died 1760), known as the *Baal Shem Tov* or *Besht*, gave Chasidism to the Jewish world. And Chasidism gave Kabbalah its widest base and most uncritical acceptance. The teachings of the *Besht* were a recipe for curing the prevailing unhappiness. The *Baal Shem* held that personal consciousness of God required the joyful exercise of the gifts of God. To reject the permitted pleasures of the senses, to wallow in sorrow, was a kind of insult to God, he proclaimed. So Chasidism celebrated God and God's works in prayer and song and dance.

The *Baal Shem* left no written record of his ideas; his disciples and followers recorded all he said—or all that they said he said. And they carried the *Besht's* message from his small town in the Ukraine throughout eastern and central Europe.

Chasidism is dynastic, and wherever the *Besht's* followers settled they established a court and a dynasty. And, just as each *dynast* or *rebbe* had his own approach to Judaism, so each put together his own unique combination of Kabbalah's many ideas and concepts. Some were more Lurianic than Luria; some, like *Chabad Chasidism* (represented by the Lubavitcher Chasidism) created original forms. But the central core was the same in each: a popularization of Kabbalah through simplification and literalness. In apparent paradox, Chasidism blossomed and made Jewish mysticism a living force at the same time that science and enlightenment blossomed, making rationalism the new religion for many.

The *Zohar* is too dense for most Jews who are not scholars to penetrate. *Gematria* (see Chapter 16) and other magical mysteries was the property of the adepts. Even the Lurianic Kabbalah was for specialists in some degree. However, Chasidism made mysticism attainable and acceptable to ordinary Jews by establishing a new hierarchical version of the old mystical doctrine of the elect.

The study of the esoterica of Kabbalah, the most secret knowledge, was left to the *Rebbe*—the master, the *Tsadik*—to whom the individual chasid gave fealty and obedience.

The *Rebbe* decided what had to be done. All that was required of the members of the *Rebbe's* court or congregation was obedience to the *Rebbe* and the *mitsvot*—the commandments—and true, ecstatic prayer, prayer with *devekut*. In the language of Jewish prayer, *devekut* means cleaving to God.

The *Besht* said that *devekut* through prayer had to be "in the here and now." It could not be achieved through mortification of the flesh, through fasting and denial. *Devekut* was reached by way of joyous celebration of the Divine, by joyful acceptance of the gifts with which *Eyn Sof* has adorned the everyday world.

The *Baal Shem* had the mystical idea that cleaving to God resulted in communion with God, which was more important than study. One of his disciples, Rebbe Menachem Mendel, said:

> If we divert our thoughts from devotion to God, and study excessively, we will forget the fear of heaven . . . study should therefore be reduced, and one should [instead] always meditate on the greatness of God.

Menachem Mendel's view was extreme, but mainstream Chasidism agreed with the principle. This put Chasidism on a collision course with non-Chasidic Jews, called *mitnagdim* (opponents), who placed study at the top of their religious priorities. Menachem Mendel's anti-intellectual attitude, which was so inviting to many Jews, frightened the strongly intellectual Jewish establishment. It was doubly alarming because of the historical and philosophical context. For more than a century after Shabbatai Tsevi had been shown to be a fraud, Sabbatianism continued as a heretical sect. Various Sabbatian sects, some with satanic and orgiastic practices, flourished in central and eastern Europe. The provinces of Podolya and Volhynia were centers of the Sabbatian heresy—and centers of Chasidism. The *mitnagdim* often confused the two new movements. From Vilna, the intellectual capital of Ashkenazic Jewry—"the new Jerusalem"—Rabbi Elijah ben Solomon, the *Vilna Gaon*, denounced this new anti-intellectual mystical sect, Chasidism.

Despite the opposition of mainstream Jews, Chasidism spread. It was, in a sense, a revivalist movement with all the spontaneity and mass participation common to such movements. One of its strongest attractions was its personalization of worship and practice of the *mitsvot*. These were given personal meaning by the Kabbalistic theory of the redemption or *tikkun*.

Before Chasidism became powerful enough to threaten the Orthodox establishment, there had been relative peace between traditional Jews and followers of mysticism, say, between 1500 and 1800. During this period, traditionalists welcomed the Kabbalists as a positive force, and mystical practices penetrated deep into the customs, ethics, mythology, and religious practices of normative Judaism.

Mystical prayers were added to the daily service, giving new meaning and depth to the prayer experience. Following the Safed Kabbalists, the Sabbath was celebrated as the mystical union of the bride *Shechinah* and the groom God. The Safed Sabbath eve custom of reciting the verse from Proverbs that begins "A woman of valor . . .," became universal. The Kabbalistic idea of the transmigration of souls, its version of the world-to-come, and its angelology became part of Jewish folkways. Mystical-magical practices became commonplace. (Not all of these beliefs, practices, and superstitions came out of Kabbalah; many were co-opted from Christian central European neighbors.)

Since, according to Kabbalah, fulfillment of the commandments is a necessary first step toward freeing the soul to rise, and only the soul of a strongly ethical person can achieve union with the *sefirot*, Jewish ethics incorporated the Kabbalistic concept of *tikkun*, or redemption and repair. *Musar,* the Jewish ethical movement of the nineteenth century, incorporated Kabbalistic notions of ethical conduct and in turn became a major part of the teaching program of Chasidic yeshivot.

With Chasidism, Kabbalah was no longer an esoteric discipline limited to a select few, its practice mainly speculative and meditative. Every Chasid was, in a way, a Kabbalist. Mainstream Jews began to pray with Kabbalistic prayers and follow Kabbalistic practices, unaware of their source.

16

STUDY QUESTIONS

1 What was the contribution of Chasidism to Kabbalah? According to the Chasidim, who was best able to study and interpret the *Zohar*?

2 What is *devekut*? How can one achieve it?

3 Who were the *mitnagdim*? Why did they strenuously oppose the spread of Chasidism among Jews? Where was the center of their movement, and who was their principle leader?

4 Under the influence of Chasidism, how did Kabbalah penetrate normative Judaism?

5 Read a short biography of the *Baal Shem Tov* (for example, in the *Encyclopedia Judaica*). What were some of his major teachings? Why did he not compile his own writings?

The Kabbalists' Universe

THERE IS NO SINGLE normative Jewish theology. Ideas of God, creation, Torah, Law, prayer, evil, and Providence vary with Ashkenazim and Sephardim; with German and Polish Ashkenazim; with Turkish Sephardim and Oriental Jews; among Orthodox, Conservative, and Reform Jews. And Jews of local rites—Yemenite, Bokhari, Roman, etc.—may differ with all the above.

Extensive variation was just as much the pattern with followers of Kabbalah. Spanish, German, African, and Palestinian Kabbalists differed; and within the same geographical area mystics differed over time. From the second century to the twentieth, Jewish mystics have tried to experience God in their own ways. Each used all manner of techniques, ranging from the purely spiritual and speculative to the practical and magical. But regardless of time and place, all Jewish mystics have started their speculative journeys from a common point with a common view of God and man's relationship to Him. All agree that:

— *God cannot be known.*

— *God is both transcendent—separate, above and beyond all else, not limited by time or space—and immanent—indwelling completely within all creatures. Kabbalists appear more interested in God's immanence than His transcendence.*

— *There is within God the desire to be known.*

— *There is within God the desire to create.*

— *God did not create the universe from nothingness.*

✳ — *Man is created in the likeness of God. By moving away from Godly attributes—justice, mercy, compassion, love, and so on—man has defaced that image.*

— *The mystic's task is to rebuild that image, to bring it once again close to God's semblance.*

— *The mystic begins his search by doing what God commands, by faithfully fulfilling God's commandments. Faithful obedience to the Law brings the human likeness closer to God's likeness, thus healing the defaced image of man.*

From this set of givens, Kabbalists tried to penetrate the basic mysteries, to find answers to seemingly unanswerable questions: How could an infinite Being create a finite universe? How could a perfectly good and totally omnipotent God allow evil to exist? How could a just and merciful God allow (condemn?) the Jewish people to suffer a very long and very painful exile?

Speculation produced explanations, varying with time and place. Some were simple and naive, others complex and sophisticated. Some early ideas were disregarded along the way, others expanded. Many were embellished from non-Jewish sources—for example, the angelology and demonology was adapted from the Zoroastrian Avesta texts learned during the exile in Babylonia and Persia.

Over the centuries a Kabbalist's picture of the universe and its creation emerged. The last major refinement of the mystical explanation of creation was that of Isaac Luria and his Safed followers. This was the version accepted and embellished by Chasidism. The Lurianic story of Creation answered some age-old questions; it also answered questions of burning importance to 16th and 17th century refugees from Spain: Why the Exile? How could God allow the expulsion of the Jews from Spain? In view of these cataclysmic events, what is the Jews' vocation in this world?

Again the warning that must precede all Kabbalistic descriptions: This story of creation is not offered as a description of what actually happened. It is impossible for human beings to know such things. So the story is figurative, a metaphor, not to be taken literally. This metaphor for the beginning of all is limited in two respects: Although the events described did occur in heaven, the story is told from a human perspective, and divine elements are described in human words. Yet how else can human beings communicate with each other? As the *Zohar* puts it, "All this is said from our point of view, and it is relative to our knowledge" [*Zohar* II, 176a].

According to the Safed Kabbalists, creation was not a necessary consequence of God's nature or essence. God could have done otherwise. But according to the mystic's view, there is within God a desire to create. A desire, not a need. (How can God have needs?) So creation was, metaphorically, God's decision, an act of Divine Will. It is improper to ask why God made this decision because any possible answer would involve ideas and concepts totally beyond human understanding.

The difficulty in applying the word "why" to God illustrates the basic problem in explaining mystical ideas and concepts to rationalists. To speak of God "acting" or of "God's will" is wrong; it applies human concepts to God. Yet these are the only instruments we have to describe what is by its nature indescribable and undefinable.

Despite limitations, the Kabbalists drew a metaphorical picture of the process and history of creation.

Their picture begins, as all things must, with God, God as *Eyn Sof*, Without Limit, Infinite, Everywhere. It is impossible to imagine any place that is not God since the existence of such a place would mean that God is limited, not infinite. We are left with the paradox of an Infinite God and a finite universe side by side.

This paradox is resolved by the concept of *tsimtsum*, the contraction. In the mystical story of creation, God withdrew into Himself; He concentrated His essence. A space appeared, called *tehiru*. This primordial space, not outside of God but within Him, makes possible the existence of something other than God. In effect, the *tsimtsum* is the self-limitation of God.

When philosophers argued that you couldn't have both Divine ubiquity—everywhereness—and *tehiru*, non-God space, the Kabbalists offered an analogy: Take a deep breath. Gather together within yourself all your breath. Hold it. You now have within yourself a bubble of air, a space. Without lessening yourself you have created within yourself a place that is not you, a kind of *tehiru*.

God expressed the idea of creation; He expressed His will to create. And in the space, the *tehiru*, appeared Adam Kadmon, the primordial man. Adam Kadmon is an emanation of the creator aspect of God. Adam Kadmon is a light, the first and highest of the *sefirot*. Out of Adam Kadmon flow other lights, other emanations; in all, nine *sefirot* in addition to the first *sefirah*.

The word *sefirot* is from the Hebrew verb *safar*, to enumerate. In Kabbalistic literature, the *sefirot* are the 10 stages of emanations from God, each a manifest action of the various attributes of God. Since the human mind deals most easily with physical concepts, the sefirot are generally thought of—and spoken of—as "lights." The sefirot are divided into upper lights—the first three sefirot—and six lower lights. The six lower sefirot serve as the principle instruments of Creation. The tenth sefirah, the Shechinah, is necessarily different from the others because it is directly involved in and touches the world of being.

At the Creation each light, each sefirah, was contained in a vessel, much as an ocean is contained within the bowl of its shores. The vessels containing the upper lights were strong and held the mighty power of the sefirot they embraced. But the vessels that held the six lower lights could not contain their power. They shattered. The shattering of the vessels was the shevirah.

In the shevirah the vessels containing the lower sefirot broke into myriad pieces, shards. In this heavenly explosion, the shards were exploded into the cosmos. These shards, called klipot (shells or husks) captured sparks of the unquenchable light released by the shevirah. Combined with the celestial light, the klipot took on shape and substance and gained enormous power. Because the klipot were the products of the shevirah, of destruction rather than creation, their power is evil; they are the dark side of creation. Evil became a reality and a force in the created world through the klipot.

There are variations in this description of creation, differences in details but not in essentials. In one, the lights did not emanate from Adam Kadmon, but directly from Eyn Sof into the 10 vessels. The vessels gave each light, each sefirah, an individual character. However, the lights were too intense, too strong, too heavy, to be contained in the vessels. The vessels shattered. The lights that formed the top three sefirot flowed back to Eyn Sof; the others flowed into the void. Some sparks of the divine light clung to the shattered pieces of the vessels and fell downward.

The shevirah, the shattering of the vessels, was the decisive crisis of all divine and created being. In it the very process of creation was upset; the levels of creation were pushed apart. Even the male and female aspects of God were displaced. Since that cataclysm, nothing in time, in place, or in order is where it was supposed to be in the Divine plan of creation. A thing or a being not in its proper place is in exile. Thus, as a result of the shevirah, that moment-of-creation event, all created beings are in exile. Centuries after this version of creation first surfaced in Jewish mystical circles, modern scientists came up with their version of the shevirah. They call it the big-bang theory of the beginning of all things.

Everything in heaven has its reflection here below; all events in this world are reflections of events on high. Scripture records earthly parallels to the heavenly tsimtsum and shevirah. The tsimtsum was a negative act, a withdrawal, and thus a forerunner of exile. Adam's fall in Scripture corresponds to the shevirah. When Adam sinned, he was exiled; his great soul was shattered, reduced to sparks. Because of Adam's fall, the Shechinah, the tenth sefirah, the bridge between this world and the world above, was also shattered into sparks. The mingled sparks of Adam's soul and the shattered Shechinah are prey to the husks and shells, the klipot. And so, evil is abroad in this world.

The above is written in the past tense; God withdrew; the vessels shattered; the klipot burst, etc. It would be equally correct to write it in the present tense because for Jews, creation is a constant, ongoing, unending process.

The Kabbalist's story of creation does not end on this despairing note. If it did, it would mean that creation had no positive purpose. This is impossible for a

God with the attributes of goodness, mercy, and justice. There is a third great critical event: the *tikkun*. The *tsimtsum* and the *shevirah* were heavenly events of the primordial past. *Tikkun* is in the now and in the future. The *tsimtsum* and the *shevirah* occurred in the upper world. *Tikkun*, although in the desire of heaven, is in the hands of man.

Tikkun is mending; *tikkun* is healing; *tikkun* is redemption. On high, the *sefirot*—those healing, constructive lights—continue to issue from Adam Kadmon. They do half of the work of *tikkun*, the heavenly half. This leaves to humanity a vital part in the great restoration of wholeness.

Why us? Because human beings are the apex of creation; because we were created with free will. The endpoint of *tikkun*, the final healing, will be reached when evil is defeated and human beings bring themselves back to *Eyn Sof*'s intention. *Tikkun* will be accomplished when we are once again "the image of God."

In order for *tikkun* to take place, the *klipot* must be dissolved and the evil residing in them eliminated. This requires love and mercy on the part of people, as these qualities are the solvents of the *klipot*. When the great *tikkun* has been accomplished, the exile of the Jews and the mystic exile of the *Shechinah* will be over. Only then will there be a true conjunction of male and female—in the upper world in the aspects of God, on earth between human beings.

God has from the beginning offered us opportunities for redemption, for the great *tikkun*. Jewish history is a record of the victories and defeats in this process. Adam could have achieved it, but he failed by sinning. The revelation on Mount Sinai gave the Jews another opportunity; they failed when they rejected God and turned to the golden calf. But God is patient as well as good, so He continues to offer to every human being the opportunity of *tikkun*.

Torah is the instrument of *tikkun*; it is the map and guidebook to *tikkun*. Every person who acts according to Torah sends a spark of the shattered vessel of the *Shechinah* home to heaven. Every act in fulfillment of the Torah sends heavenward the spark of *Adam Kadmon* that resides in every human being. The duty of *tikkun* falls on us individually and collectively. Each individual Jew has a personal role to play in this process. Each Jew, by cleaving to God, helps cleanse the world of the demonic *klipot*. Collectively, Israel moves the whole world toward the great *tikkun*, toward the Messianic Age, by accepting the Torah, by following Jewish law.

STUDY QUESTIONS

1 Discuss the areas of agreement which Jewish mystics share. In what ways do these fit with the general definition of mysticism found at the beginning of this text?

2 Describe the process of creation as Isaac Luria taught it. Why did the vessels shatter? How could God contract to create the primordial space and still remain everywhere?

3 Identify the following terms:
(1) *Sefirot*, (2) *shevirah*,
(3) *tsimtsum*, (4) *Shechinah*,
(5) *klipot*, (6) *Eyn Sof*, (7) *tehiru*,
(8) *Adam Kadmon*, (9) *Zohar*,
(10) *tikkun*.

4 Explain the partnership involved in the mystical explanation of Creation. What part is played by God through the upper *sefirot*? What part is played by human beings through the lower *sefirot*?

PART TWO

**Selections from
the Sources
with Commentary**

Secrets of Torah

Zohar III, 152a

"THE LORD SPOKE TO Moses in the wilderness of Sinai, on the first new moon of the second year following the exodus from the land of Egypt, saying: Let the Israelite people offer the Passover sacrifice at its set time . . ." Num. 9:1-2.

Rabbi Abba said: Why was the command regarding the paschal lamb repeated here after it had been given to them once before while they were in Egypt? The reason is that the Israelites thought that the first command was intended only while they were still in Egypt and not for future years. The command was renewed in *the second year* to tell them that it was to be kept throughout the generations. *In the first month of the second year* contains a sublime mystery. The month signifies the moon and the year points to the sun that sheds light upon the moon. This was the position when all the laws of Torah were delivered to Israel.

Rabbi Simeon said: Alas for the man who sees in the Torah only stories, and reads the Torah as dealing with everyday matters. If this were so, anyone could make up an even better Torah dealing with ordinary things. Princes already have better books that deal with things of this world, which we could use as a model for a worldly torah. But the Holy Torah has within it heavenly secrets and divine truths. *"And this is what Guido said as well."*

Come and see: The upper world and the lower world are in perfect balance. Israel, below, is balanced by the angels, above. Of the angels on high it is written: *He makes the winds His messengers [angels]* Ps. 104:4. Angels are spirits [winds] and when they come down to earth they must put on earthly garments. If they didn't have a physical covering, they could not remain on earth, nor could the earth hold them. If this is true of angels, how much more true is it of the Torah, for the Torah created the angels, as well as all the worlds—all of which continue to exist only because of the Torah. So, too, with the Torah itself: the world could not contain the Torah unless she were clothed in some earthly form.

The stories in the Torah are its earthly outer garments. Woe to those who mistake this outer garment for the essential Torah itself, for they will be denied a share in the world to come. As David said: *[Lord,]open my eyes that*

I may behold wondrous things out of Your Torah Ps. 119:18. This refers to the mysteries which are under the Torah's outer covering.

NOTE

Come and see! A fool looks at a man and sees mainly his clothing, and judges thereby. But, in truth, the shape of a person's clothing merely suggests the significance [shape] of the body inside. Moreover, that body has significance only because of its soul.

So it is with the Torah. The "body" of the Torah is made up of the precepts of the Torah. (The Hebrew expression is *gufei-Torah, guf* meaning body or principle, thus the translation, "bodies of the Torah.") These are clothed in the tales of the Torah which tell of this world. Fools see only the stories, the trappings, and do not know that there is substance under the surface. Those with greater understanding can perceive the body under the outer stories. The truly wise, those who serve the Highest, those who stood at Sinai, see all the way through to the soul, to the root principles of the true Torah. In the Next World, these [truly wise] will be able to see the soul of the soul of the Torah.

Come and see! Thus it is in the worlds above the world: outer garment, body, soul, soul-of-soul. The outer garment is the heavens and all they contain; the body is the community of Israel; the soul is the Glory of Israel; and the soul of the soul is the Ancient Holy One. All these are entwined one within the other.

Woe to the wicked ones who see the Torah only as a collection of tales dealing with things of this world; who see only the garment and seek no further. Happy are the righteous ones who see the Torah as it really is. Just as wine must be contained in a bottle, so the Torah can be held only in a garment of narratives—which it is our duty to penetrate.

THE ZOHAR IS in the form of a commentary on Scripture by Rabbi Simeon bar Yochai and his companions. Like most commentators, they did not restrict themselves to the text under examination but ranged far afield—often very far afield. In this selection, Rabbi Simeon and his companions begin with an explanation of Numbers 9:1-2, the verse that legislates for all time the celebration of Passover. This is dealt within one paragraph, followed by an explanation of the nature of Torah and the relationship between the world above and the world below.

Underlying Rabbi Abba's explanation of the apparent repetition of the laws of Passover is a Jewish tradition cited in the Talmud: Rab Judah said . . . "*Of all that the Holy One, Blessed be He, created in His world, He did not create a single thing without purpose.*" Shabbat 77b. Applying this statement to Torah, we learn that there are never any empty repetitions in Scripture, no superfluous words. Every word, being of divine origin, is of divine importance. What may appear to be a repetition is really a new idea, often with hidden meaning.

Many of Rabbi Simeon's discourses open with the phrase *Rabbi Simeon patach* . . . This translates literally: "Rabbi Simeon opened" [his explanation of this verse of Scripture]. The great chasidic sage, Rebbe Pinchas of Koretz, gave a more imaginative translation: "Rabbi Simeon opened this verse." That

24

is, Rabbi Simeon opened to human view the "divine truths" to be found within this verse. An example of opening the Torah is the explanation of the esoteric meaning of the Passover ordinance.

The literal reason for the apparent repetition of the commandment to celebrate the Passover is given first: The repetition ensures that the ordinance is obeyed forever. Only then is the sublime mystery of the repetition uncovered: The mystery lies in the references to the moon and the sun. In Kabbalah, the moon is represented by the *sefirah malchut*; the sun by the *sefirah tiferet*. On the eve of Passover, the moon and the sun, and their *sefirot*, are in the positions they were in when the Torah was given to Israel—in the aspect of revelation.

Kabbalah is a logical system, and like all logical systems it begins with a set of givens. In this case, the givens are the same set of basic premises that underlie all Jewish intellectual and theological structures: God is; God is One; the Torah is God's revealed Word. These premises accepted, the logical reasoning is this: Since God is infinite and ultimately incomprehensible to humans, it follows that anything about God is also infinite and incomprehensible to humans. Torah is the Word of God, and is, therefore, incomprehensible to us. However, the Torah was offered to humans. Therefore, parts of it—levels of it—must be understandable to us.

On the surface, Scripture is history, prophecies, stories, ordinances, rules of conduct, philosophy. But if that were all, says Rabbi Simeon, the book would not be unique, perhaps not even as good as many existing books: "Princes already have better books that deal with the things of this world [alone] . . ." (In the time of Moses of Leon, the literate few knew the books of Homer, the geometry of Euclid, the ethical-legal works of the Greek philosophers. What makes the Torah different—what makes it holy—is its divine origin, its "heavenly secrets and divine truths." To most of us, these are the "incomprehensible" aspects of the Torah.

The work of the mystic is to uncover the mystery behind the Word. The great mystics—those who are righteous and "truly wise"—can unravel these mysteries down to the very soul of the Torah. In the world to come, the righteous will see even further—into the incomprehensible essence of Torah—to the soul of the soul. Torah is unlike the books of worldly princes for Torah has many inner dimensions of mystery and meaning.

This idea flows from another basic principle of the Kabbalah: All things of this world are reflections of the things of the world above. Reflections, not copies. Consider the reflection in water of a man lighting his pipe. Neither the man nor the fire could exist in the water, yet they are there in the reflection. So it is with the things of the heavenly world; they are reflected in this world but they themselves cannot exist in this world. For example, an angel, pure spirit in the world above, its natural habitat, cannot exist in this world. Nor can this world contain an angel as pure spirit. When an angel comes to this world in obedience to the command of heaven, that angel must be clothed in "this-worldly" garments. It assumes an earthly body.

So it is with the Torah; it, too, had to be clothed before it could be given to this world. The garment on the Torah is formed of its stories, precepts, and prophecies. Deep within this garment are the Torah's hidden truths. Just as a person's clothes only hint at the shape of his body, and the shape of his body doesn't give a clue to the nature of his soul, so the stories—the Torah's "clothes"—hint at the precepts, the body of the Torah. Within the body are the root principles, the Torah's soul. Still deeper within is the soul of the soul.

The way to understanding, to uncovering the mysteries, is not open to every-

one, not even to the apparently wise. The road is open only to the elect, to those who have prepared themselves properly. The prerequisite for becoming eligible to uncover the hidden mysteries of the Torah is to accept, and faithfully and fully obey, the commandments—the *mitsvot*—required by the literal words of the Torah. The commandments are a guide to the good life here on earth; they lead to peace and harmony here, the necessary first step in communicating with God.

What is the mystical process by which the *mitsvot* link the human soul to God? According to Kabbalah, the commandments are found in the Torah and so stem from heaven. Therefore, each commandment is suffused with supernal light. When a human fulfills a commandment, the light of that commandment touches the soul of the person doing the *mitsvah*. The light of the fulfilled *mitsvah* touches a human soul at one end and the heavenly light at the other. The joined lights of hundreds of commandments form a pathway from earth to heaven.

Although the *mitsvot* define the Jew, they are not a Jewish preserve. Within them is the hope of the entire world. If Jews, individually and collectively, follow the 613 commandments, as is their special obligation, the entire world is brought closer to the great *tikkun*, the final redemption.

The 613 commandments are never listed as such in the Torah. Some are stated distinctly: *You shall not murder* Deut. 5:17. Some are extensions of God's words: *Be fruitful and multiply, and replenish the earth* Gen. 1:28, i.e., marry and have children. Still others are clothed in the tales of the Torah. However, say the wise man, there are precepts and mysteries located within and beyond the simply-stated and simply-clothed *mitsvot*. Those learned in the mysteries of Kabbalah keep searching to see all the way through to the soul, to the root principles of the hidden Torah.

1 Explain the following statement: "The stories in the Torah are entirely necessary. Without them, Torah could not exist in this world!"

2 How does the *Zohar* suggest that we properly "prepare" ourselves to fully understand the Torah?

3 How is the "community of Israel" simultaneously (a) linked to the world above, and (b) the hope of this world?

4 The commentary suggests that there are four ways of discovering the full complement of 613 commandments in the Torah. (a) What are these four ways? Using a copy of the Torah, try to find examples of the first three kinds of *mitsvot*. (b) Describe the fourth way.

Mystery of Creation

Chayim Vital, *Ets Chayim* 1:2

KNOW THAT BEFORE THERE WAS any emanation and before any creatures were created a simple higher light filled everything. There was no empty space in the form of a vacuum, but all was filled with that simple infinite light. <u>This infinite light had nothing in it of beginning or end but was all one simple, equally distributed light.</u> <u>This is known as "the light of *Eyn Sof*"</u> [Without End, The Infinite].

There arose in His simple will the will to create worlds, and produce emanations in order to realize His perfect acts, His names, and His attributes. This was the purpose for which the worlds were created.

Eyn Sof then concentrated His being in the middle point, which was at the very center, and He withdrew that light, removing it in every direction away from that center point.

Then there remained around the very center point an empty space, a vacuum. This withdrawal was equidistant around the central empty point, so that the space left empty was completely circular. It was not in the form of a square with right angles, for <u>*Eyn Sof* withdrew Himself in circular fashion, equidistant in all directions.</u>

The reason for this was that, since the light of *Eyn Sof* is equally spaced out, it follows necessarily that His withdrawal should be equidistant in all directions, and that He could not have withdrawn Himself in one direction to a greater extent than in any other. It is well known in the science of mathematics that <u>there is no more equal figure than a circle.</u> It is otherwise with a square, which has protruding right angles; or with a triangle, or with any other figure. Consequently, <u>the withdrawal of *Eyn Sof* had to be in the form of a circle.</u>

Now, after this withdrawal of *Eyn Sof* (which left an empty space or vacuum in the center of the light of *Eyn Sof*, as we have said), there remained a place in which there could emerge the things to be emanated, to be created, to be formed and to be made. There then emerged a single straight line of light from His circular light, and this came in a downward direction, winding down into the empty space.

The top end of this line derived from *Eyn Sof* and touched Him, but the bottom end of this line down below does not touch the light of *Eyn Sof*.

By means of this line the light of *Eyn Sof* is drawn down to extend itself down below.

Into that empty space He caused to emanate—He created, He formed, and He made—all the worlds.

Before the emergence of these four worlds, *Eyn Sof* was One and His Name One in a wonderful mystical unity of a kind beyond comprehension even to those angels nearest to Him. For the mind of no creature can comprehend Him since He has neither place nor limit nor name.

IN DESCRIBING CREATION, the Torah says: "God said, 'Let there be [light, day, creatures etc.]' . . . and there was . . ." Scripture says nothing about *how* it all came into being. This was enough. Apparently, the *how* problem troubled neither the composers of the *aggadot* and *midrashim* nor the early mystics, a thousand years after the canon of Torah was closed.

The collection of *midrashim* called the *Pirkei de Rabbi Eliezer*, written in the eighth century, considers the *why* of the creation of the world, but not the *how*. According to Rabbi Eliezer's midrash, when God resolved to create the world, He took counsel with the Torah, which had already been created. The Torah advised that a king needed an army, courtiers, and attendants. Lacking these, over whom would the king rule? Who would give him homage? Ordinary earthly kings would have these attributes of power; certainly the King of Kings deserved more. There were two lessons in this teaching: God needs us as much as we need Him; and for earthly rulers: heed His example, consult your advisers before doing anything important.

In the thirteenth century, the intellectual climate of Moslem Spain demanded more sophisticated answers. The *Zohar*, a product of that time and place, explained not only *why*, but *how* creation took place:

The world was created through the agency of the *sefirot*.

Three centuries later, when the Lurianic Kabbalah was developed, Copernicus had already created a revolution and Galileo was about to confirm it. This was the age of great geographical exploration, a search for sources, questioning what had hitherto been accepted as truth—an age in which the *Zohar*'s story that the world had been created through the *sefirot* wasn't enough. Creation through *sefirot* was acceptable, but where did the *sefirot* come from? Luria and his disciples answered this question with the *tsimtsum, shevirah, tikkun*. These concepts moved the *how* of creation back to the absolute beginning.

With their reconstruction of the Kabbalah, the Safed mystics also answered more immediate sixteenth century questions, questions Jews were asking seriously for the first time: Why us? Why the Jews? Why the Exile? What is the Jews' vocation in this world? This selection from Chayim Vital's *Ets Chayim* (*Tree of Life*) describes the initial phase of creation, the very beginning of the beginning, the *tsimtsum*.

The section opens with a description of the supernal light: "Know that before there was any[thing] . . . a simple higher light filled everything." Light is a primary symbol in most religions; some even worship it in the form of fire or the sun. In Judaism, light is a symbol of the divine, the symbol of all that is good and all that is holy. The *sefirot*, the emanations of God, are seen as lights.

The lights of the *mitsvot* connect individual souls to heaven. "For the *mitsvah* is a lamp, and the Torah is a light" Prov. 6:23. In the *Pesikta de-Rab Kahana*, God says, "I desire to create the world by means of light." And in the *Zohar* [III, 31a]: "Israel is a wick, Torah is oil, and the *Shechinah* is light."

According to the *Ets Chayim*, light is the basic ingredient in creation. However, not all light is Light. The difference is described in the Talmud: The Light created at the very beginning was not the same as the light of the sun, moon, stars [which were created on the fourth day]. A person—had there been one in the early days of creation—would have been able to see to the end of the world by that primary Light. God hid that primeval Light from the world that He created because He knew that later generations would be unworthy. But the heavenly Light is not lost to us forever; it will reappear in the world-to-come for all the pious to see.

Vital begins his description of the first step in the Creation, the *tsimtsum*, with this supernal Light. Just as readers of Kabbalistic texts must keep in mind which kind of light is meant, so must they be wary of words such as *up* and *down*, *above* and *below*, *vacuum* and *straight line*. There are no such directions or things in the place-that-is-not-this-place; no up and down, no above and below, no air or airlessness. Human beings have no choice but to use these words, but in mystical texts these words are metaphors for concepts beyond human perception.

(It is much easier for our generation than it was for earlier generations to accept such words as up and down as symbols rather than reality. We have seen astronauts in space for whom up and down are purely arbitrary concepts.)

It is much the same with the Kabbalah's use of *before* and *after*, as in, "Know that before there was any emanation . . ." God does not exist in time, He is outside of time, as is His creative activity. There was no before as we understand a sequence in time. Some modern philosophers accept time as a kind of artifact, and some scientists can deal with time as a dimension, but these concepts are beyond most of us. Most of us can't even comprehend the much more physical concept of a universe of space that folds in upon itself. These words are symbols; they are metaphors for dimensions, actions, and events beyond description by our limited vocabulary. Words are poor tools for describing spiritual reality.

There is a similar problem with the idea of God's *will* to create worlds. God doesn't "will"; God doesn't "want." These words have no meaning when applied to God. This doesn't mean that creation was a happenstance, an accident. Creation was purposeful, which means it had to have begun with an idea, a "wanting" to create. Vital circumvents ascribing will to God by making the statement doubly indirect: "There arose in His simple will the will to create." Not very satisfactory, but that was the best he could do within the limits of human language.

The Lurianic Kabbalah's version of creation begins with two givens, two facts that we have to accept unproven. Accepting a basis of unproven givens is not contrary to the rules of logic, even Euclidian geometry begins with such givens, called axioms. Axioms are what Aristotle called statements "the truth of which it is not possible to prove." The axioms in the Lurianic story of creation are the existence of God and God's light.

The first problem dealt with in the Kabbalah's explanation of creation is sort of theological-scientific: God is both immanent and transcendent. These terms are most easily explained by saying that God is both in everything and outside of everything. That's why the Kabbalists call God *Eyn Sof*, The Infinite, The Limitless One. Infinite and finite are absolute opposites; they cannot co-exist. The existence of a finite universe implies the existence of a place which is non-God. How can this be? The Kabbalists offer the *tsimtsum* as the answer: God withdrew, He contracted, leaving a space that appears to be non-God. In this non-Godly space, a finite universe would be created.

In terms familiar to sixteenth century logicians and mathematicians, Vital explained why this non-God space is necessarily circular: In a non-circular space, the distance from center to points on the perimeter would vary. God would be further away from the center in one direction than in another. This would be contrary to God's attribute of equal justice. So the space left by the *tsimtsum*—called *tehiru*—had to be a perfect circle.

Another troublesome idea: In our world, darkness is the absence of light; it occurs naturally when light is withdrawn or extinguished. But in the mystic's view, darkness is a substance, a created substance. When the supernal light was withdrawn, the *tehiru* was filled, not with darkness, but with nothingness, chaos.

Into the *tehiru* emerged "a single straight line of light from His circular light [the light outside the circle of *tehiru*] . . . down into the empty space," to the center point of the space. "The top end of this line touched Him, but the bottom end [which touched the center point] did not touch the light of *Eyn Sof*." This made creation possible within the *tehiru*. (Think of this light as that which brings order out of chaos rather than as a chaser of darkness.)

✱ In the Jewish scheme of things, nothing can exist without connection to God. The line of light connected creation (of a finite world) to God. As the line of supernal light stretches from the edge of the circle to the center of the *tehiru*, it gets further and further from God. The light is less and less of God as it moves from edge to center. At the center it is sufficiently distant from the supernal light for creation to be possible.

This line of light is transformed into emanations, lights. These are the *sefirot*, the agents of creation, not the author of creation. Although they are heavenly entities, they are not holy. Holy entities are outside of time; the *sefirot* operate in this world, and anything of this world is in time.

The basic questions of how an infinite God could create a finite universe and how the power of God could be exerted in a non-Godly space have now been answered to the Kabbalist's satisfaction.

An odd notion is introduced at the end of this selection from *Ets Chayim*. In the non-Godly space, the *tehiru*, "He made all the worlds." There is an old tradition, set down in a midrash in *Bereshit Rabbah*, that ours is not the first world created by God. There are many legends about former worlds; all say that they were destroyed because they were either imperfect or did not have the potentiality for perfection. This world isn't perfect either, but it is within the power of human beings to make it so. Even this world was almost destroyed because God's original intention was for it to be a world of absolute justice. However, when God saw that a world of absolute justice would be unstable, He added an equal measure of mercy: "There is no true justice unless mercy is part of it" [*Zohar* IV, 146b].

30

STUDY QUESTIONS

1 The selection deals with two basic problems confronting the Kabbalists. First, how can there be a world if God's Presence fills all space? Second, how can God be separate from the world and yet a part of it? Leaving mysticism aside for the moment, how does traditional Judaism answer these problems?

2 Explain the theory of *tsimtsum*. What of God is left in the vacuum created when God withdrew from the universe?

3 What are the two axioms which are the necessary points of departure for belief in Luria's theory of creation?

4 Light is a central building block in mystical thought. Even the *sefirot* are considered "emanations of light." How does Vital explain the differences between the light which we see by in this world and the Light which belongs to God?

The Vessels

Zohar II, 42b

. . . WOE TO THE MAN WHO PRESUMES to compare the Lord with any attribute, even one which is His own, much less any human created form, "whose foundation is in the dust" Job 4:19 and whose products are frail . . . soon vanishing, soon forgotten.

The only idea of the Holy One, blessed be He, which man dare to conceive, is of His sovereignty over some particular attribute or over creation as a whole. He has to be seen this way because there is no attribute, or similitude, or form which can otherwise apply to Him. This can be compared to the sea, whose waters have neither form nor tangibility in themselves, but only when they are spread over a vessel, like the earth.

On this basis, we can view it thus: The source of the sea is one. A current forms in the sea . . . which is *Yud*. The source is one, and the current makes two. A great basin is formed, . . . dug in the earth, which is filled by the waters which come from the source. This basin, which we call sea, is the third entity. This large basin is split into seven channels, like so many rivers. The waters flow from the sea into the channels. The source, the current, the sea, [and] the seven channels number ten. If the Master who made these channels should break them, the waters return to their source, and nothing remains but the dry, waterless, broken channels.

In like manner, the Source of sources brought forth the ten *sefirot*—calling the source *crown* (*keter*), an inexhaustible fountain of light—which is why He designated Himself "*Eyn Sof*," Limitless, Without End. He has neither shape nor form; there is no vessel to contain Him, no means to comprehend Him . . .

Then He made a vessel [as] small as the letter *Yud*, which is filled from Him, and called it wisdom-source . . .

Afterwards, He made a large vessel, and called it *sea*, and designated it as *understanding* (*binah*).

He is both *wise* and *understanding* in His own essence. Wisdom does not stand by itself, but only through He who is wise and has filled it from His fountain. Understanding does not stand by itself, but only through He who filled it from His essence. If He were to separate Himself from them, they would be empty, arid. It was about this that it was written, "As the waters fail the sea, and the flood decays and dries up" Job 14:11. Also, "He smites [the sea] into seven channels" Isa. 11:15.

[Then] He diverted [His essence] into seven precious vessels, called "Greatness," "Strength," "Beauty," "Victory," "Majesty," "Foundation," and "Sovereignty" . . .

All things are in His power, whether he wills to decrease the number of vessels, or increase the light that springs from them . . . However, above Him there is no god who could increase or lessen.

Then He created beings to minister to these vessels: one throne supported by four columns, with six steps leading to the throne; ten in all. The whole throne is like the cup of benediction . . . in harmony with the Torah which was given in ten words [the Decalogue] and with the ten words by which the world was created. He prepared angelic hierarchies for the throne to serve Him: *melachim* [angels], *erelim, seraphim* [seraphs], *chayot* [living beings], *ophanim, hamashalim, elim, elohim* [heavenly beings], *bene elohim* [sons of heavenly beings], *ishim* [supernal men].

THIS SECTION BEGINS with another warning not to confuse an aspect of God with God Himself: God may be merciful, but God is not Mercy; God is omnipotent, but God is not Omnipotence. The strongest warning is against substituting for God an object created by human beings, something "whose foundation is in the dust [of this world]." No thing, entity, or person created by God—not even the *sefirot*—are to be put on the same plane as God.

There are special warnings against thinking of or treating the *sefirot* as divine. "Wisdom [the *sefirah* of *chochmah*] does not stand by itself. . . . Understanding [the *sefirah* of *binah*] does not stand by itself. . . . If He were to separate Himself from them, they would be empty, arid."

✶This idea of the absolute Oneness of God, the idea that nothing and no one approaches His majesty, is fundamental to all Judaism; it is not specifically Kabbalistic. However, Kabbalists had more to worry about in this area. Their explanations of the nature of creation included entities that were closer to the Heavenly Throne than were human beings, so humans were tempted to ask for the help or

intercession of these otherworldly creations, the *sefirot*. Then too, while most Kabbalists practiced speculative Kabbalah—dealing mostly with ideas, meditations, prayer states, etc.—there were practical Kabbalists who dealt with magic and other things which existed somewhere between the world above and the world below. Warnings against invoking these heavenly beings had to be—and were—repeated and repeated.

God is so different in kind that even God's Name may not be pronounced. This rule stems in part from awesome respect—even earthly kings and queens are addressed by title or attribute, not by name—and, in part, from fear.✶There is a kind of magic in a name, and, in some sense, a kind of power over the named. Adam's dominion over the other creatures was confirmed when God paraded all the animals before him so that Adam could name them.

✶God's Name, first used in Scripture in Genesis 2:4, is spelled *Yud, Hay, Vav, Hay*. These four letters are referred to by scholars as the Tetragrammaton, from the Greek *tetra*, four, and *grammat*, letter.

God doesn't use His Name in Scripture. When Moses first asks God to reveal His Name, God answers: "*Ehyeh Asher Ehyeh*" Exod. 3:14. This is either translated, "I Am that I Am," or "I Am what I Will Be," or not translated at all. When the Tetragrammaton appears in Scripture, it is the word *Adonai* that is read aloud. As the Talmud states, "The Holy One, Blessed be He, said: I am not called as I am written. I am written with a *yud, hay* [*vav, hay*], but I am read, *aleph, dalet* [the first two letters of the word *Adonai*]" Kiddushin, 71a.

Adonai is only one of the titles used to avoid God's own name. Other frequently used substitutes are:

El—*The oldest used word for God, meaning Power* (as in Gen. 33:20).

Elyon—*Most High God* (Deut. 32:8)

El Olam—*Everlasting God* (Isa. 40:28)

El Shaddai—*God Almighty; literally, God of the [Cosmic] Mountain* (Gen. 17:1).

El Ro'i—*God Who Sees Me* (Gen. 16:13)

Eloha, Elohim—*Lengthened form of El* (Gen. 20:13).

Elohim, Elohim Chayim (the Living God), and *Adonai* are plural forms, but do not denote plural gods. Some scholars say the plural form is used as a mark of deep respect, as in the plurals associated with royalty. Others say the plural form is a grammatical construct similar to the plural forms of other abstract words. For example: *chayim* (life); *zekunim* (old age), *ne'urim* (adolescence).

Having warned us that *El*, and *Adonai*, and *El Shaddai* describe a single aspect of God and do not in any way represent His totality, this portion of *Zohar* moves on to the next stage of creation.

Its out of the light that connects God-Light to the center of the *tehiru* that the *sefirot* emanate. They are not yet separate, but a mingled essence of God-attributes—wisdom, power, judgment, beauty, etc. These emanations flow into channels generally referred to as vessels. In the vessels the *sefirot* take on individual characteristics.

There are two references to *yud* in this section: as the *source* and as "a vessel [as] small as the letter *yud* . . . wisdom-source." *Yud*, the smallest letter in Hebrew (it is shaped like a comma), has great mystical-magical significance in the Kabbalah. It is the first letter in the Name of God; it is also the number ten (in the old Hebrew counting system, wherein letters are used for numbers) which has great mystical importance.

The different trends in Kabbalah have different ideas of what happened after the *sefirot* were given shape by the vessel. All versions agree that the vessels were unable to carry the enormous power of the emanations. They shattered. This *shevirah*, or breaking of the vessels, a central idea in the Lurianic Kabbalah, is the heavenly catastrophe of which exile is the worldly counterpart. The *shevirah* is also the source of evil. This great tear in the original plan of creation can be healed by *tikkun*, only by the actions of human beings—the creatures created in the likeness of God.

STUDY QUESTIONS

1 God is unique, totally different from everything else in the universe. In what way do the names we use for God show our inability to comprehend God?

2 How do human beings form an essential part of the *tikkun* of the universe?

3 In what ways has the number ten (represented by the Hebrew letter *yud*) played an important part in your study of *Zohar* thus far? What other "tens" play important parts in Judaism?

34

The Sefirot

Tikkunei Zohar, Second Introduction

ELIJAH BEGAN TO praise God, saying:

Lord of the universe, You are One, but not numbered. You are Higher than the highest. You are the mystery above all mysteries. No thought can grasp you at all. It is You who produced the Ten Perfections, which we call the *Ten Sefirot*. With them you guide the secret worlds which have not been revealed and the worlds which have been revealed, and in them You conceal Yourself from human beings. But it is You who binds them together and unites them. Since You are in them, whoever separates any one of these ten from the others—it is as if he had made a division in You.

These *Ten Sefirot* follow the order of long, short, and medium . . . This is the order they follow: *Chesed* [lovingkindness] is the right arm; *Gevurah* [power] is the left arm; *Tiferet* [beauty] is the torso; *Netsach* [victory] and *Hod* [splendor] the two legs; *Yesod* [foundation] is the mouth, which we call the Oral Law. The brain is *Chochmah* [wisdom], the inner thoughts, *Binah* [understanding] is in the heart, and of it we say: "The heart understands." Regarding these latter two [*Chochmah* and *Binah*], Scripture says: "The secret things belong to the Lord our God" Deut. 29:28.

The elevated *Keter* is the crown of sovereignty, and of it Scripture says: "Declaring the end from the beginning" Isa. 46:10. It is the skull upon which the *tefillin* are placed. From within it is *Yud, Hay, Vav, Hay* [the unsayable Name of God], which is the way of emanation. It provides the water for the tree—its arms and its branches—just as a tree grows when it is watered.

Lord of the Universe! You are the Cause of causes, the Ground of grounds, Who waters the tree by means of a spring—and that spring is the soul of the body by which the body survives. In You there is no likeness or image of anything within or without.

You created heaven and earth and produced in them sun, moon, stars, and planets; and upon the earth, trees, plants, the Garden of Eden, animals, birds, fishes, and human beings, in order that through them the upper worlds can be known, and it can be known how the upper and lower worlds are controlled and how the upper and lower worlds can be recognized.

35

No one can know anything about You. Apart from You none is unique, and there is no unity apart from You in the upper and lower worlds. You are known as Lord of all there is. Among all the *sefirot*, each has a special name by which angels are called. But You have no special name, for You fill all names, and You are Perfection of them all; and when You remove yourself from them, all names remain as body without soul.

You are wise, but not by means of a known wisdom. You understand, but not by means of a known understanding. You have no known place except to make known Your power and might to human beings, and to show them how the world is controlled by judgment and mercy—which, according to the deeds of men, are righteousness and justice. Judgment is the same as Power. Justice is the same as the Middle Pillar. Righteousness is the same as Holy Sovereignty. "Just Measures" are the same as the Two Pillars of Truth. The "Just *Hin*" [fair measure] is the same as the Sign of the Covenant. It is all for the purpose of demonstrating how the world is controlled . . .

THIS PORTION OF THE Lurianic addition to the *Zohar*, known as Elijah's prayer, is an example of the pervasive influence of Kabbalah upon normative Judaism: Although a part of the *Zohar*, Elijah's prayer is included in many standard prayer books as part of the morning prayers.

The prayer describes the *sefirot*, which are, in the Kabbalah's view, basic to the relationship between *Eyn Sof* and the created world. God is neither comprehensible nor knowable to human beings; therefore, it makes no sense to wonder or to speculate about God's nature. However, God does reveal aspects of God's self through the *sefirot*, so most Kabbalistic speculation centers on these emanations.

As with all Kabbalistic descriptions, the method is by metaphor and symbol. The *sefirot* are emanations of divinity, for which light is a metaphor; in another metaphor, they are likened to a tree. Yet they are most often described as the figure of a man—Adam Kadmon. A single *sefirah* may be imagined as part of the metaphoric human figure or tree, but we are constantly cautioned that *Chesed* is not an arm, *Keter* is not the head, etc. That is to say, such descriptions are not to be taken literally; they are to be understood only "as if."

The idea of the emanations was probably borrowed from the major Neoplatonist philosopher Plotinus (third century C.E.). However, Plotinus' theory of emanations was quite different from that of the *sefirot* of the Kabbalists. The Neoplatonists saw the emanations as a middle stage between the Absolute One and the physical world. In a sense, Plotinus' emanations were outside and unconnected to the One. For the Kabbalists (in this case Rabbi Elijah), the *sefirot* are not interposed between God and created beings; rather they are fundamental aspects of God through which the divine light moves in the created world.

Elijah's prayer starts with the statement that God is "One but not numbered." That is, when the word "one" is used in relation to God, it is not the same as the number one. The number one is followed by two, followed by three, etc.; it is part of a series. But One applied to God is an absolute; nothing else exists or can exist on the same plane, nothing can follow One. God is "Higher than the highest."

Elijah refers to the *sefirot* as the Ten *Tikkunim*, here translated as the Ten Perfections. *Tikkun* has the meaning of amending, healing, redeeming; and so, of perfecting. It is in that sense that Elijah calls the *sefirot* the Ten Perfections.

From early on, Jews pondered on—and worried about—the balance between mercy and justice (or judgment). They understood that neither quality could exist without the other. True justice could not exist unless it was tempered by mercy. In fact, the former worlds were destroyed because they lacked the necessary balance of both qualities. It is in this sense that the *sefirot* are described as following "the order of long, short, and medium." Long refers to mercy; short, to judgment; medium, to a balance of the two qualities.

The *sefirot* are divided into triads or groups of three. Each set of three includes a "long" *sefirah*, which has the quality of mercy; a "short" *sefirah*, with the aspect of judgment, and a harmonizing "medium" *sefirah*. The last *sefirah*, the one closest to this world, is not part of a triad.

The order in which the emanations are named in Elijah's prayer is not the order of descent. They are enumerated here as parts of the anthropomorphic Adam Kadmon, as we would list the parts of the body. In proper order of closeness to the realm of God, they are:

1. Keter, or Crown. *Also called the Simple Point, the Ancient of Days, Adam Kadmon.*
2. Chochmah, or Wisdom. *The primordial idea of God, also called Abba or Father.*
3. Binah, or Understanding. *The intelligence of God, also called Imma or Mother.*

This is the first triad, representing mental and intellectual qualities. It is in this first tier of *sefirot* that their sexual aspect is introduced. This is in keeping with a statement in the *Zohar*: "When the Holy One gave definite form to everything that exists, He made things in either masculine or feminine form."

4. Chesed, or Lovingkindness. *The mercy of God, also known as Gedulah, or Greatness.*
5. Gevurah, or Power. *Also called Din, Justice.*

6. Tiferet, or Beauty, Glory. *Also called Rachamim or Compassion.*

This is the middle triad, representing moral qualities. Chesed is feminine, Gevurah is masculine. Tiferet combines the two and thus mediates between justice and mercy.

7. Netsach, or Firmness, Might, Victory. *The lasting endurance of God.*
8. Hod, or Splendor. *The majesty of God.*
9. Yesod, or Foundation. *The basis of God's active force.*

The third triad represents spiritual qualities and, in a sense, the physical. *Netsach* is masculine, *Hod* is feminine. *Yesod* is the mediating combination.

10. Malchut, or Kingdom. *This sefirah represents the world of matter, the funnel through which the qualities of the upper sefirot are transmitted to the physical world. Malchut is also Shechinah, the most feminine aspect of God, the most approachable of His emanations, the one closest to us. The word Shechinah is from the Hebrew shechan, to dwell: "The divine presence dwells in her."*

The names of the *sefirot* are suggested in a Scriptural verse that lists aspects of God:

Thine, O Lord, is the greatness, and the power, and the glory, and the victory, and the majesty, for all that is in heaven and in the earth is Thine; thine is the kingdom, O Lord, and Thou are exalted as the head above all" 1 Chron. 29:11.

Each emanation is an individual, with individual characteristics, powers, qualities, even color. Yet they are a unity and cannot be separated—another of the many paradoxes in the Kabbalah. Like most Kabbalistic enigmas, this paradox can be explained by an "as if": The *sefirot* are like a single flame reflected in ten mirrors, each of a different color. The light is seen as ten lights, yet the ten are one. Herein

This is what SABA meant when He described a woman as a chalice created by G-d.

37

lies the meaning of the warning that anyone who separates "any one of these from the others—it is as if he had made a division in You."

The imagery of the *sefirot* as a human figure is from Genesis 1:26: "And God said: Let us make man in Our image, after Our likeness . . ." The figure of Adam Kadmon, the primordial man both human and beyond human, represents the first *sefirah*, *Keter*; this *sefirah* is both the whole figure and a part of that figure. In the mystical account, great lights shine from Adam Kadmon's eyes. The lights are the *sefirot*, and the *sefirot* are the symbolic Adam Kadmon. (Remember "as if"!)

The first *sefirah*, *Keter*, is the head; more specifically, the skull of Adam Kadmon, the part that wears the *tefillin* (phylacteries) as a crown.

Chesed, mercy, is the right arm of Adam Kadmon, and *Gevurah*, which is also *Din*, justice, is the left arm. In most cultures, including Judaism, the right arm is symbolic of greater strength than the left. So it is that in the symbolism of Adam Kadmon mercy is given greater strength than justice.

Tiferet , glory, which combines Justice and Mercy, is also *Rachamim*, compassion. It represents the center, the torso. *Binah*, understanding, is within the torso; it is the heart.

The two legs which hold up the mighty figure are *Netsach*, firmness, and *Hod*, majesty.

The basis of the relationship of human beings to God is the covenant, and the mark of the covenant is circumcision. So *Yesod*, foundation, is represented by the genitals.

Malchut, sovereignty, is the mouth, representing the Oral Law, which explains the Written Law. *Chochmah*, wisdom, is, of course, the brain.

The use of Adam Kadmon as a representation of the *sefirot* is more than a device to give the limited human mind a

hint of the reality of divine light. It also has a theological purpose: The ten *sefirot* make up—and so influence—the human-like Adam Kadmon. They also influence human beings, Adam Kadmon's counterparts in this world. The laws of both physics and theology say that for every action there is a reaction; If the *sefirot* can influence human beings, human beings can influence the *sefirot*, and in turn the upper world.

This is the reason human beings— and no other created creatures—were given free will. Humans have the power to improve (perfect) this world. Since the lower world is merely a reflection of the upper, when we advance our world toward *shalom* (peace or wholeness) we move the upper world closer to the state of wholeness that existed before the *shevirah*. However, free will also has a negative potential: humans have the ability to do evil. If they do evil, they create dissension and disruption in this world that has a like effect in the world above.

Adam (this world's Adam, of Adam and Eve) was responsible for disrupting the harmony of creation, but his descendants have the power to restore the harmony through *tikkun*. By using the commandments of the Torah as a guide, human beings can help move this world into the state of harmony that was the original intention of God.

All this is implied in the statement:
You have no known place except to make known Your power and might to human beings, and to show them how the world is controlled by judgment and mercy—which are righteousness and mercy [Gevurah and Chesed, combined as Tiferet], according to the deeds of men . . . . It is all for the purpose of demonstrating how the world is controlled.

Our simplest actions, particularly how we fulfill the commandments, are important in affecting the things of this world, which in turn influence the world of the *sefirot*. This is emphasized by the reference to "just *hin*." The commandment to give fair measure (*hin*) in the marketplace is much more than a commandment not to cheat. Each of the 613 commandments has an affinity for a specific *sefirah*, the commandment of "a just *hin*" is directly involved with the *sefirah* *Yesod*. In the metaphysical Adam Kadmon, *Yesod* is the genitals, the sign of the covenant. There is another lesson here: Read Scripture carefully and deeply; every verse has within it a truth about the world above.

The reference to the names of angels in this excerpt is to the custom of calling some angels by the names of the *sefirot*. Jewish mystics took the idea of angels much more seriously than normative Judaism.

STUDY QUESTIONS

1 The Talmud states that if the world were judged by God's attribute of justice alone, it would be destroyed, as were other worlds before this one. Why has our world survived?

2 Nine of the ten *sefirot* are divided into groups of three. Explain the three groups and their division. There is also an inherent division of the *sefirot* into two groups—higher and lower. Tell which five are in each group.

3 Explain the importance of the following verse from Genesis (1:26): "And God said: Let us make man in Our image, after Our likeness . . ."

4 Draw a stick figure of Adam Kadmon, and label the parts of the figure according to the explanation given in the commentary. According to the Kabbalah, what does Adam Kadmon represent?

Spirit and Soul

Zohar I, 83a

RABBI SIMEON, HIS SON Rabbi Eleazar, Rabbi Abba, and Rabbi Judah were on a journey. As they went along, Rabbi Simeon said: I wonder at how men can be so indifferent to the words of the Torah and the problems of their own existence! He then spoke on the text: *At night I yearn for Thee with all my soul; yea, with the spirit within me I seek you early* [in the morning] Isa. 26:9.

He said: The inner meaning of this verse is that when a man lies down in his bed, his vital spirit [*nefesh*] leaves him and begins to mount upwards, leaving with the body only the heartbeat contained within the impression of a vessel. The spirit tries to mount from level to level; in doing so it meets certain bright, unclean essences. But if the spirit [of the sleeping man] is pure, if it was not defiled during the day, it rises above the seductive, unclean essences. But if the spirit is not pure, it becomes entangled with the unclean entities and does not rise above them.

Dreams These essences show the spirit certain things that will happen in the near future; sometimes they delude the spirit and show her false things. Thus the *nefesh* goes about all the night and when the man awakens, she returns to her place [within him].

Happy are the righteous to whom God reveals His secrets in dreams, so that they may be on guard against transgression! Woe to the sinners who defile their bodies and their souls! As for those who have not defiled themselves during the day, when they fall asleep at night, their souls begin to ascend and enter first those levels which we have mentioned [where the unclean essences entice]. However, the pure spirits do not cleave to [these unclean essences] and continue to mount further. The soul which is privileged to rise finally appears before the gate of the celestial palace and yearns with all its might to behold the beauty of the King and to visit His sanctuary. This is the soul of the man who will ever have a portion in the world to come ... Therefore it is written: "At night I yearn for Thee with all my soul"; [that is,] to follow God and not be seduced by false powers. These words refer to the soul, or *nefesh*, which has sway by night, while the words "with the spirit within me I seek You" refer to the spirit, or *ruach*, that has sway during the day.

40

Soul [*nefesh*] and spirit [*ruach*] are not two separate grades [inferior and superior], but are on a single level which has two aspects. There is a third aspect which should dominate these two and cleave to them as they to it. It is the higher spirit, [the] *neshamah*. This higher spirit, the vessel, the man, is called holy, perfect, wholly devoted to God.

Soul [*nefesh*] is the lowest stirring; it supports the body and feeds it [spiritually]; the body is closely connected to this spirit. When it is sufficiently qualified [free of evil], it serves as the throne on which rests the lower spirit [*ruach*] . . . When both [*nefesh* and *ruach*] have prepared themselves sufficiently, they are qualified to receive the high spirit [*neshamah*], for which *ruach* serves as a throne. Thus there is a throne resting on a throne and a throne for the highest.

From observing these grades of the soul, one gets an insight into the higher Wisdom, and it is wholly through Wisdom that certain mysteries are connected together. For *nefesh* is the lowest stirring to which the body cleaves, like the dark light at the bottom of a candle-flame that clings to the wick and exists only through that wick. When this light is fully kindled, it becomes a throne for the white light above it. When both dark light at bottom and white light above are fully kindled, the white light becomes a throne for a light which cannot be fully described, an unknown something resting on that white light. Together there is formed a complete light.

RABBI SIMEON EXPLAINS here the three mystical stages or levels of the human soul: *nefesh, ruach, neshamah*. He makes the point that these divisions of the soul, which he calls "grades," are equal; one is no more important than another. Yet, as many traditional writers do, Rabbi Simeon treats the divisions as though they were graded: *nefesh* on the lowest step, *ruach* higher, *neshamah* highest.

According to one tradition, the *nefesh*, the source of our individual physical and psychological functioning, is with us at birth. *Ruach* becomes part of our being at the moment we become aware that we have souls; that is, when we begin to study Torah, follow the commandments, and ponder the mysteries to be found therein. To a Jew, it is self-evident that knowledge of Torah leads inevitably to obedience to the commandments.

There is a parallel here to a *midrash*: children are born with the *yetser hara*, the evil inclination, but do not achieve the *yet-*

ser tov, the inclination for good, until about the age of puberty (*bar and bat mitsvah*).

Although Simeon doesn't use the word dream here, the reference to "when a man lies down in bed" and the spirit leaves the body can only refer to a dream state. (*Zohar* may avoid saying dream because of the Jewish dispute about the meaning and authority of dreams.)

In the Scriptural view, dreams are heavenly communications. Joseph was told in a dream that he would rule over his brothers (Gen. 37:5). Jacob was warned about the descent into Egypt when "God spoke to Israel [Jacob] in the visions of the night" Gen. 46:2. Some prophets received their divine messages in dreams, and were warned not to withhold such messages from the community: "A prophet that has a dream, let him tell a dream; and he that has My word, let him speak My word faithfully" Jer. 23:28.

Some sages of the Talmud were far more hard-headed: "A man is shown in a dream only what is suggested by his thought" Berachot 55b. However, like most statements in the Talmud, this one is hotly debated. One of the sages, Samuel, didn't take any chances:

When Samuel had a bad dream, he used to say, "dreams speak falsely" Zech. 10:2. When he had a good dream, he used to quote "I [God] do speak with him in a dream" Num. 12:6.

When it was pointed out to Samuel that his position was a contradiction, he said, "There is no contradiction; in the one case [of a good dream] it is through an angel, in the other [the bad dream] it is through a demon" Berachot 55b. Rabbi Meir held that "dreams neither help nor harm" Horayot 13b. Still, many Jews fasted when they had bad dreams, hoping to avert the dire premonitions.

While Maimonides accepted the Talmud's statement that "dream is one-sixtieth of prophecy" Berachot 57b, he also seems to have dismissed it in a scholarly analysis:

You are . . . acquainted with the activities of the imaginative faculty [including memory], such as retaining and combining the impressions of the senses, and its natural propensity to imitation, as well as the fact that its greatest and noblest activity takes place just when the senses are at rest and do not function [during sleep] . . . Guide, II, 36.

In effect, Maimonides held that dreams are a function only of the imagination, that we can learn nothing new from dreams, and that they arise from sensual and sensory impressions buried in the "imaginative faculty."

Not every Jewish scholar agreed with Maimonides, but Maimonides' view remained the dominant one. It was confirmed in the late nineteenth century when a responsum said that "one should take no notice of dreams because we know that [they are] not in heaven."

One scholar who disagreed with Maimonides' view of dreams caused a centuries-long dispute among Ashkenazic Jews. In the thirteenth century, Ephraim of Regensburg, a noted Talmudist, was asked to judge whether sturgeon is *kosher*. After due reflection, he decided that sturgeon is *kosher*, but while asleep that night, Ephraim dreamed that sturgeon is not *kosher*. The next day he reversed his day-old decision.

The *Zohar* gave importance to dreams, but not as absolutely as it gave importance to Torah. While indicating that dreams are close to prophecy, Kabbalah set more store on the dreamer than in the dream: the dreams of the righteous are likely to come true; the dreams of the wicked are probably snares.

This is the view found in this section of the *Zohar*. When we sleep, the soul leaves the body and rises into a realm of evil *klipot*. If the *nefesh* is pure—not defiled by wrongful acts—it rises above the unclean essences. If the body is not pure, the *nefesh* becomes entangled with evil, and the information in such a dream is false.

We must now go back to the beginning before the beginning, to the cataclysmic pre-creation event: the *shevirah*, the breaking of the vessels. When the vessels shattered, unable to hold the enormous power of the lights of God's emanation, shards of the vessels remained, flying loose in the spiritual cosmos. Most of the light, no longer contained in the vessels, flowed back to the source, but some light remained loose in the spiritual cosmos. The shards of the shattered vessels, the *klipot*, attached themselves to these sparks of emanation-light. The shards are evil, the result of the initial exile, the first division between the world above and the world below. They became powerful by attaching themselves to the sparks of supernal light. That is why the *Zohar* describes them as "bright, unclean essences."

When the body falls asleep, leaving "only the heartbeat," the *nefesh* rises up-

42

ward and encounters the unclean essences. If the spirit is pure, if the person had not transgressed the commandments, the unclean essences cannot cleave to the *nefesh*. In its dreams, the pure spirit may see "His secrets" revealed. However, the spirit of an evildoer becomes entangled with the unclean shards. Its dreams are of false things.

There is another version of the nature of the soul in this portion of *Zohar*. In its description, the *nefesh* is "the lowest stirring," because it is most closely connected to the physical body. Only if the body is free of evil is the attendant *nefesh* pure enough to serve as the throne, which is the *ruach*, upon which sits the highest aspect of the soul, the *neshamah*. The metaphor of the candle-flame is exact.

STUDY QUESTIONS

1 Is there an official Jewish position on the meaning and significance of dreams? If so, explain the position. If not, explain why not.

2 Jewish mystics explain that dreams may be either extremely significant or utterly mistaken. How can both of these be true at the same time? What causes the two different possibilities to exist?

3 Describe the three stages of the human soul. What are the significant features of each stage?

4 In what way does the commentary relate the existence of evil to the existence of exile?

True Fear

Zohar I, 11b

"IN THE BEGINNING GOD created..." Gen. 1:1. This contains the first precept, namely, the fear of the Lord, as it is written: "The fear of the Lord is the beginning of wisdom" Ps. 111:10, and "The fear of the Lord is the beginning of knowledge" Prov. 1:7. Fear of the Lord is the beginning and the gateway of faith, the foundation of the world.

There are three types of fear: two are false, having no proper root; the third is the real fear. First is the man who fears the Holy One, blessed be He, so that his children will live and not die. He is in constant fear for his possessions and his body. Obviously, this is not genuine fear of God. Second is the man who fears the Holy One, blessed be He, because he is afraid of the punishments of the other world, of the tortures he would receive in *Gehinnom*. This, also, is not genuine fear. Genuine fear is that which a man has who knows that He [God] is a mighty King, the rock and foundation of all worlds, before whom all created things are as nought, as it is written: "And all the inhabitants of the earth are as nought" Dan. 4:32. This man's goal is that spot called fear [*yirah*]....

Here, below, there is a "holy fear" and there is an "evil fear".... Now, he whose fear is of punishment and accusation does not have the fear of God, which leads to life. His fear is the evil fear of the lash, but not the fear of the Lord. For this reason, the spot which is called "the fear of the Lord" is also called "the beginning of knowledge." This precept is laid down here because it is the root principle of all the other precepts laid down in Torah. In effect, He who does not cherish this fear does not observe the other precepts of the Torah, since it is the gate to them.

... The second precept is love, and is indissolubly bound up with the first, the precept of fear. A man should love his Master with a perfect love, with the love called "great love." This is implied in the command "Walk before Me, and be wholehearted" Gen. 17:1, meaning love. It is also implied in the verse, "And God said, Let there be light" Gen. 1:3, which refers to perfect love.

Rabbi Eleazar said: Father [Rabbi Simeon], I have heard a definition of perfect love ... It is the love which is complete through the union of two aspects ... There is, for example, the man who loves God because he has

44

riches, long life, children, power, success in all his undertakings, which form the reason for his love of God. Should the Holy One, blessed be He, turn the wheel of fortune against this man so that he suffers, this man will change, and his love will disappear. This is a love without root. Perfect love remains steadfast in affliction as well as prosperity. The right way to love one's Master is expressed in the traditional teaching: "Even if he deprive me of my life . . .."

―――

FROM THE EARLIEST days, Jews experienced a tension between love of God and fear of God and often confused the two. The Torah, reflecting more primitive notions of the proper human response to God, emphasized *yirat Elohim*, fear of the Lord. In the Talmud, written many centuries later, love and fear of the Lord are given equal emphasis. As if to mark the change, the Rabbis generally speak of *yirat shamayim*, fear of heaven, rather than *yirat Elohim*.

Fear of God and fear of heaven are not to be confused with fear of punishment or with fear of losing God's bounty. As this portion of *Zohar* illustrates, proper fear of heaven is not based on fear of pain or loss, fear of going to *Gehinnom* [an evil place, a kind of Jewish hell]. Perhaps reverence—respect so deep that it becomes awe—is a better word than fear for what the Lord requires of us. *I agree* ᵖ.ᵉ.

For instance, the commandment: "If there be among you a needy man . . . you shall not harden your heart, nor shut your hand from your needy brother; but you shall surely open your hand to him . . ." Deut. 15:7,8. If you feast while your neighbor goes hungry, you have violated the commandment, but if you feed your neighbor because you are afraid that you will end up poor, or that you will go to hell, you have not fulfilled the commandment properly. Your motivation was not fear of the Lord.

In *Sifra*, a collection of *midrashim* on Leviticus, the meaning of fear of the Lord is delimited. Fear of God, says *Sifra*, does not refer to transgressions that might be known to others—stealing, selling spoiled

goods, etc.; there are judicial and social penalties for these crimes. "You shall fear your God" refers to sins "known [only] in the heart," sins for which community sanctions are unlikely because these sins are known only to the person committing them. Examples would be turning away when passing someone in need of help, not going to visit a sick neighbor, etc. Support for this reading is found in the language of Leviticus, the book that lists the laws of proper conduct for a Jew, such as "Love your neighbor as yourself" Lev. 19:18.

Many of the *mitsvot* enumerated in Leviticus end with the statement: "I am the Lord your God." The authorship of the law is reason enough to obey it. But some of the laws end with a double admonition: authorship and fear. "You shall not curse the deaf, nor put a stumbling block before the blind; but you shall fear your God, I am the Lord" Lev. 19:14. "You shall rise up before the hoary head, and honor the face of the old . . . and you shall fear your God, I am the Lord" Lev. 19:32. "You shall not wrong one another; but you shall fear your God; for I am the Lord" Lev. 25:17.

The *mitsvot* with the "fear your God" addition have a common feature: they are the secret commandments, *mitsvot* whose transgression would be known only to the transgressor—and to God. The deaf do not hear his curses; the blind do not see who put the stumbling block before them. Transgression is known only "in your heart"; there can be no social or communal penalties. You obey these commandments only because "you fear your Lord."

reverence

45

"And you shall cleave to Him" Deut. 13:4 expresses the ultimate goal for all mystics, and fear of the Lord is an essential ingredient in cleaving to God. For Jewish mystics, the path to this cleaving is through *devekut*, a combination of prayer, meditation, and study so intense and concentrated that the soul is carried to ecstatic heights.

For centuries mystics debated whether *devekut* is best reached through love or fear. The debate is purposely not resolved, for to choose love over fear, or fear over love, would make true *devekut* unattainable. Love means closeness, and you do not fear that which is lovingly close. Fear implies power, greatness. You do not fear that which has no power to harm you. You want to distance yourself from that which you fear. Since God is both as close as our hearts and as distant as heaven, the Kabbalah balances love and fear.

Central to the idea of fear and love of God is the concept of free will. The Torah teaches that God "requires" fear and love. In this statement "requires" is used in the sense of "wants"—God wants us to fear Him and to love Him. The Lord could have created human beings with the love and fear built it—just as angels and the heavenly host were created incapable of *not* loving God—but humans are given free will. They have a choice: they are free to love (or fear) God; they are free not to love (or fear) God. They may follow the commandments, or they may not. Heaven has no power to force either decision; it is up to the individual human being. The Sages said, "Everything is in the hands of heaven except the fear of heaven" Niddah 16b. We pray for the strength to do as God wants, to love Him. In the traditional morning prayer we ask God to "unify our hearts to love and fear Your Name."

The love and fear we ask for is not merely an emotion or a state of mind,. Love and fear are verbs as well as nouns.

Applied to God, they must be verbs. Moreover, the verbs must be active, they must require doing something. In this case, it is doing the will of God.

STUDY QUESTIONS

1 What three types of fear exist in people? Which of these is the true fear of the Lord, and why?

2 What do the commandments which end with "you shall fear your God, I am the Lord" have in common? What special significance do they have for the mystics?

3 Explain the meaning of the talmudic statement, "Everything is in the hands of heaven except the fear of heaven."

4 What is "perfect love"? How does this precept balance the precept of fear?

Secret Knowledge

Yosher Divrei Emet, Chapter 22*

    MY HOLY TEACHER, RABBI Menachem Mendel, blessed be his memory, taught that the term *nistar* [secret; also used as a term for Kabbalah] is applied to something you cannot explain to someone else. For example, since it is impossible to describe adequately the taste of a food to someone who has never eaten it, this is called a "secret" word. The same is true of the love and fear of God. It is impossible to describe to someone else the feeling of love in your own heart, and thus it is called "secret." How is it possible then to say that the teachings of the Kabbalah are secret? After all the book is there for anyone who wants to study it; a person who cannot understand what he reads is ignorant, and if that were the kind of person we were talking about, we might as well say that the Talmud is "secret."

    The genuinely secret element in the *Zohar* and in the writings of Rabbi Isaac Luria is that they are based on communion with God, and thus are intended only for those who are able to be watchers of the Holy Chariot (true mystics)—as was Isaac Luria, of blessed memory, who knew all the paths of heaven and always walked them in his mind, like the four sages who entered *pardes*.

    The difference between a person who is constantly contemplating God and one who is not is explained by imagining someone who briefly meets a stranger from another town and then does not recognize him when they meet later. He does not recognize the stranger because when they first met, the stranger's image did not register on his mind and made no impression on his memory. As a result, he cannot "unite" with the stranger when they meet each other a second time. It is as if they do not know each other. This is exactly what happens to someone who contemplates God only occasionally, when he is in the mood. He will never come to know God, or love God, or have communion with Him.

    On the other hand, someone who contemplates God constantly, or at least at every possible opportunity, is like someone who sees another person several times in different ways. The other person's image is imprinted in his heart and remains with him when the other is far away.

---

* From Joseph Dan, *Teachings of Chasidism*, pp. 49-50

BEFORE THE AGE OF PRINTING, books were laboriously hand copied, and therefore scarce. Lack of popular access to its texts was one means of maintaining the esoteric element or secret nature of Kabbalah. Printing made the *Zohar* and the Lurianic texts widely available: "After all, the book is right there for anyone who wants to study it." Yet despite the easy availability of the source books, Kabbalah remained an esoteric discipline, as this quotation from *Yosher Divrei Emet* [*True and Just Words*] explains. The mystical knowledge within the book remained secret because it was understandable only to those who knew "the paths of heaven"—the select few.

What is required of a person to penetrate the secrets hidden within the literal words is *devekut*, total communion with God. (*Devekut* is, literally, cleaving; i.e., cleaving to God.) A person who achieves *devekut*, says *Yosher Divrei Emet*, a major Chasidic text, is one who contemplates God constantly (or, at least, at every possible opportunity. The person who contemplates God, or cleaves to Him, only when he is in the mood, may be able to read the words of the Kabbalah's texts, but he will not understand their secret meaning.

The author of *Yosher Divrei Emet*, Rabbi Meshullam Feibush Heller of Zborez, paraphrases his teacher, Rabbi Menachem Mendel of Peremishlany, a disciple of the Baal Shem Tov himself. From this we know that Rabbi Meshullam Feibush is of the second generation of Chasidic masters: he is quoting a leading member of the first generation of disciples of the founder.

Chasidism was a revolutionary movement in Judaism and was thus prey to the kind of extremism that afflicts most revolutionary movements. Like many other such movements, mainstream Chasidism was tempered by success and adapted to the larger world in which it operated. Some Chasidic groups, of course, became even more extremist.

Rabbi Menachem Mendel said:

If we divert our thoughts from devotion to God, and study excessively, we will forget the fear of heaven . . . .Study should therefore be reduced, and one should [instead] always meditate on the greatness of God.

This was anathema to established Jewish religious leaders, who prided themselves on intellectual attainments. Neither was Rabbi Menachem Mendel's anti-intellectualism universally accepted among Chasidim. It was, however, popular with ordinary folk, in a time when scholars were a kind of Jewish nobility and working people had little time to study.

The deprecation of study by Chasidim eased somewhat as the quarrel between them and the *mitnagdim* [opponents; those who valued study] was relaxed. To this day, prayer and meditation are more important than study in Chasidism. The path to heaven is a secret one, and the secret is open only through total obedience to the Law as interpreted by the *Rebbe*, and total cleaving to God through *devekut*.

STUDY QUESTIONS

1 Explain *devekut*. How does one reach *devekut*? What makes *devekut* so essential within the Jewish mystical system?

2 What is the genuinely secret element in the *Zohar*? Why is this element beyond explanation?

3 What, according to Chasidism, is the proper place of study within the Kabbalah? Why did this belief give rise to heated debate and anathema between Chasidism and the *mitnagdim*?

Male and Female

Zohar I, 55b; 49b

DISCOURSING ON "Male and female created He them" Gen. 1:27, Rabbi Simeon said: Profound mysteries are revealed in these verses. The words "male and female created He them" make known the high place of man and the mystic teachings of his creation. Note that man was created in the same way as heaven and earth were created. Of heaven and earth it is written, "These are the generations of heaven and earth" Gen. 2:4; and of man it is written: "These are the generations of man" Gen. 5:1. Of heaven and earth it is written, "when they were created"; and of man it is written: "on the day when they were created . . . male and female created He them." From this we learn that every figure that does not include male and female elements is not a true and proper figure—and so we have stated in the esoteric teachings of our Mishnah.

Look: God does not accept as holy any place where male and female are not found together, nor are blessings found except in such a place, as it is written, "And He blessed them and called their name man on the day that they were created." Note that it says *them* and *their* name, and not *him* and *his* name. The male is not even called "man" until he is united with the female.

*   *   *

RABBI SIMEON SPOKE on the text: "And [Abram] went on his journeys from the south as far as Beth El, to the place where his tent had been before, between Beth El and Ai" Gen. 13:3. He said: We would expect to read "journey," instead we read "journeys" [the word has a plural ending in the Torah]. This means that Abram was not alone on this journey, but was accompanied by the Divine Presence [*Shechinah*].

A man must always be "male and female" so that his faith will remain firm and the *Shechinah* will never leave him. You will ask: What of a man who goes on a journey, away from his wife; does he cease to be "male and female"? Such a one, before starting on his journey, and while he is still "male and female" [that is, while he is with his wife] must pray to God so that the Presence [*Shechinah*] is drawn to him. After he has prayed and offered thanksgiving, and when he feels the Presence resting on him, then he can leave, knowing that through his continuing union with the *Shechinah* he will be "male and female" on his journey, just as he is "male and female" at home. For it is written, "Righteousness shall go before Him and shall make His footsteps a way" Ps. 85:14. [Scripture here uses a feminine form, *tsedek*, "righteousness."]

So while a man is away from home he should be very careful of his actions, lest the *Shechinah* leave him and the holy union be broken. [He would not longer be "male and female."] Since it is necessary [for a man] to act properly when [he] and [his] wife are together, consider how much greater is the need for proper conduct when the heavenly mate is with him. Moreover, this heavenly union is his protection during the journey. Once back home, it is his duty to give his wife [marital] pleasure, since it was she who obtained for him the heavenly partner [for his journey].

There are two reasons for this duty of cohabitation. First, this pleasure is a religious one, giving joy not only to the wife but also to the Divine Presence, for through it peace is spread in the world, as it is written: "You shall know that your tent is in peace, and you shall visit your wife in your tent and not miss anything" Job 5:24. Secondly, if his wife [of this world] becomes pregnant, the heavenly wife bestows on the child a holy soul, for this covenant is called the covenant of the Holy One, blessed be He . . ..

According to secret doctrine, men of true faith [mystics] are bound to give their whole mind and purpose to the *Shechinah*. It could be argued from the above that a man is in a state of greater holiness when on a journey than at home, because while on a journey he has a heavenly partner. This is not so. At home, the wife is the foundation, and it is only because of her that the Divine Presence resides there [and accompanies the man on his journey].

So the Sages interpreted the verse, "And Isaac brought her [Rebecca] into his mother Sarah's tent" Gen. 24:67 to mean that the Divine Presence came to Isaac's house along with Rebecca. According to secret doctrine, the heavenly Mother is together with the male only when the house is in readiness [in peace], when male and [earthly] female are truly joined. Then the heavenly Mother showers blessings on the "male and female." Similarly, when the house is prepared, and the couple joined, the earthly mother pours blessings on them.

. . . When a man is married, two females, one of the upper world and one of the lower, give him bliss, the upper one showering blessing on him, and the lower one . . . being joined together with him. But when he is on a journey, the lower [world wife] remains behind, and the *Shechinah* is still with him. Therefore, on his return, he should do that which pleasures both females, as we have explained.

PRESENT IN MANY cultures, and particularly in Judaism, is the idea that an adult person is not complete or whole without a partner. The Jewish Torah, also accepted as Holy Scripture by Christians, begins with the paired unit, and says directly that wholeness is a man/woman unity: " . . . male and female created He them. And God blessed them, and said to them, 'Be fruitful and multiply' " Gen. 1:28.

The Moslem *Koran* has a similar message: "O mankind! Be careful of your duty to your Lord Who created you from a single soul, and from it created its mate, and from the twain has spread abroad a multitude of men and women" Surah 4:1.

The notion that the male/female unity has a single soul is found in a *midrash* which explains that when a child is to be born, the angels above divide a soul and give one half to the new infant. The other half is given to an infant of the opposite sex. When these children have grown, they seek each other in order to achieve wholeness of soul. A happy marriage is that of a man and a woman whose souls are one. If they marry other half-souls, the marriage is troubled.

Zohar I, 49b, expands on this notion of wholeness, of completeness, expressed through the sexual relationship of man and wife: "There are two reasons for this duty of cohabitation. First, this pleasure is a religious one, giving joy not only to the wife but also to the Divine Presence [*Shechinah*], for through it peace is spread in the world." *Shalom bayit*, the peace of the home, which requires sexual completion, leads to *shalom olam*, the peace of the world.

Shalom, generally translated as peace, is much more than the absence of strife. *Shalom* comes from a root meaning whole, complete, sound. All of these meanings are encompassed in the term *shalom bayit*, the peace of the home and *shalom bayit* depends on "male and female." When the male/female unit is physically divided, as when the husband is away from home, is he still a whole person? Yes, says the *Zohar*, so long as there was *shalom bayit* before he left. Then the traveler has with him the close companionship of the wife's surrogate, the *Shechinah*.

But what about the other half of the male/female unit, the wife who remains at home? Neither the *Zohar* nor any other Jewish text discusses how the wife maintains wholeness when the husband is absent. The implication is that she is able to take care of herself; only the husband needs help when the male/female unit is divided.

In Kabbalah, sexual intercourse between husband and wife is seen as an earthly parallel to the mystical union of the *sefirot Chochmah* and *Binah*, of *Tiferet* and *Shechinah*. These acts, physically in this world and symbolically in the world above, promote unity, which is oneness, and *tikkun*, which is healing.

This view of marital relations as a physical, ethical, and spiritual good and a source of joy is a constant in Judaism. From the earliest days, Jews both normative and mystical held essentially the same view of marital relations as a healthy instinct, a God-given gift. Only the symbolism of the mystics set their view apart.

Despite the Jewish openness about the physical relationship in marriage, Hebrew has no word for "sex." The word *min* corresponds to the English word "sex" in the sense of gender, but there is no word which means "sex" as a physical or emotional activity. This linguistic absence is not due to prudery; sex may have to be sublimated at times, but never repressed; it is neither shameful nor sinful. The Jews just didn't talk explicitly about the physical relationship in marriage; it was an integral, a very necessary part of a total relationship. In fact, sexual activity is considered a way of channeling the *yetser hara*, the evil inclination, to constructive ends. According to the Rabbis: "Were it not for the evil inclination, no man would build a house and marry" Bereshit Rabbah, 9:7.

The term "evil inclination" used in this *midrash* does not imply that sex is evil. Every human being has two inclinations, one toward good (*yetser tov*) and one toward evil (*yetser hara*). But the actions arising out of these inclinations are not necessarily totally good or totally evil; the results might just as correctly be termed holy and earthly, or spiritual and physical. It is this earthly expression of the *yetser hara*—physical desire—that prompts us to marry and to build habitations for our families.

In his writing on the subject, Maimonides followed Aristotle, who put marital relations on a lower and less spiritual plane than, say, intellectual activity. The Rambam's view was disputed a century later in what is perhaps the authoritative work about sex, *Iggeret Ha Kodesh* [*The Holy Letter*]. This anonymous thirteenth century Kabbalistic work emphasized the importance of proper physical relations between husband and wife as an earthly reflection of the mystical union of *Chochmah* and *Binah*. Proper sexual union in this world helps promote unity in the upper world. The sexual act is, therefore, holy.

Iggeret Ha Kodesh places two important conditions on the sexual relationship in marriage. First, sex without the woman's consent is absolutely forbidden. Second, without mutual enjoyment, the act is considered profane.

Normative Jewish religious practices rooted in Kabbalah give expression to Kabbalah's sexual element. The symbolism of *Lecha Dodi*, a Kabbalist hymn chanted as a prelude to the Friday evening service, is quite specific: "Beloved, come to meet the bride; beloved, come to greet Shabbat." The custom of reciting Proverbs 31, "A woman of valor," is another Kabbalist innovation.with definite sexual overtones. (To be absolutely fair, by the time of the Talmud normative Judaism had already included the recitation of the frankly sexual Song of Songs as a part of the synagogue ritual.)

Zohar I, 49b and 55b (quoted above in reverse order), deal with the complex relationship of physical and spiritual love. A man needs a wife and a woman needs a husband. Individual fulfillment, completeness, enjoyment, requires two individuals in close communion. When a man must absent himself from wife and home, the *Shechinah* serves as his other half: "On a journey he has a heavenly partner." But this is true only if there is love and peace at home. If the man's actions either at home or on the road are improper, "the *Shechinah* [will] leave him, and the holy union [will] be broken." The reference is always to the mate; it is assumed that the woman will always act properly.

The man/*Shechinah* unity is not on a higher or holier plane than the man/woman unity when he is at home. If anything, it is the opposite. " . . . The wife is the foundation, and it only because of her that the Presence [*Shechinah*]" goes with him on his journey. Nor is it enough that he merely have a wife; the wife is the foundation only when the house is whole, when *shalom bayit* reigns.

(*A note:* The pronoun for the Torah is she, feminine, Torah being a feminine noun. The pronoun for the Lord is He, masculine. God is masculine, but the Word of God, and the *Shechinah*, the *sefirah* that connects this world and the world above, are feminine. It could be said that the idea is masculine, the operating principles are feminine.)

STUDY QUESTIONS

1 Explain the statement found in *Zohar* I, 49b: "There are two reasons for this duty of cohabitation. . . ."

2 What is the *Shechinah*? Why does the *Shechinah* accompany some men on their "journeys," while it does not accompany others?

3 What is the mystical relationship between *shalom bayit* and *shalom olam*?

4 Describe the *yetser tov* and the *yetser hara*. In what ways can the *yetser hara* be turned to good purposes?

Slander—
Intended to prove Malicious
Once you compromise your thought, mediocrity set in....
Written word — read, people believe — must be responsible...!
November 11, 2008.

52

The Power of
the Hebrew Letters

Zohar I, 55b

"ADAM KNEW HIS WIFE again, and she bore him a son, and called his name Seth" Gen. 4:25. It is to Seth that all the generations which have survived in the world, and all the truly righteous of the world, trace their descent.

Rabbi Yose said: As a result of Adam's transgression, the letters of the alphabet were reversed, except for the last two letters, which were left in their proper order. When Adam repented, he grasped at the last two letters [*shin* and *tav*] and made of them a name for the son that was born in his likeness. Despite Adam's repentance, the other letters remained in reverse order until Israel stood before Mt. Sinai [and promised to obey God's Law], whereupon the letters recovered their proper order as on the day heaven and earth were created, and the earth was once more firmly established.

Rabbi Adam said: On the day that Adam transgressed the command of his Master, heaven and earth were nearly uprooted from their place, since they were based only on the covenant, as it is written: "But for My covenant with day and night, I had not set the statutes of heaven and earth" Jer. 33:25. Adam broke the covenant, as it is written: "And they, like Adam, have transgressed the covenant" Hos. 6:7. Had God not foreseen that Israel would one day stand before Mt. Sinai to confirm this covenant, the world would have come to an end.

Rabbi Chezkiah said: See now, when God created the world, He made this covenant and established the world upon it, as it is written "*Bereshit* [in the beginning]," which we interpret as *bara sheet*, "He created the foundation"; that is, the covenant upon which the world rests. It is also called *sheet* because it is a trough from which blessing flows to the world. Adam broke this covenant and removed it from its place. This covenant is symbolized by the small letter *Yud*, the root and foundation of the world.

When Adam repented and begot a son, he called his son Seth. He did not dare to insert the *Yud* and call him *Sheet*, because he had broken the covenant symbolized by that *Yud*. However, God made Seth the father of the future generations and made him the ancestor of all the righteous who have lived since.

Note that when Israel stood before Mt. Sinai, there entered between the letters which make up *sheet* and Seth [both are written with the letters *shin* and *tav*] the letter *bet*. Thus God gave Israel the word *Shabbat* [the Sabbath; *shin, bet, tav*], as it is said: "And the children of Israel shall keep the Sabbath . . . as a perpetual covenant" Exod. 31:16. In this way these two letters achieved their original power, which had been suspended until the world returned to its whole state, and the covenant entered between them.

Rabbi Yose said: Not only were these two letters [*shin* and *tav*] fully reinstated through the letter *bet*, but also all the letters began to return to their proper order with the birth of Seth, and by the time Israel stood before Mount Sinai, they were fully restored. Rabbi Judah said: They had already been restored below [in this world], and in every generation these letters held the world together, even though they were not yet properly fixed in their places; but when the Torah was given to Israel, then everything was put right.

WE TAKE IT FOR GRANTED today that with a few strokes of a pen we can communicate love to someone far away; with a few strokes on a typewriter we can order a house built; with a few strokes on a computer keyboard we can transfer millions of dollars from here to there. But to our ancestors, the transmission of intelligence, emotion, or money by the mark of a stylus on a wet clay tablet or the stroke of a pen was a mystery. Mystery is the beginning of magic.

The king's authority was represented by a symbol impressed on wax; the high priest's authority was symbolized in a talisman. The powers that made kings and priests, so much greater than lesser folk, were contained in pieces of writing. This had to be some magic!

That a piece of writing could have enormous power was even more real to Jews than to other peoples. Jews didn't have statues, idols, or icons to represent God. All they had was something put in writing. The Jews had a Book, a Book that, according to Jewish tradition, came into being even before the world was created. While they didn't worship the Book, it was obviously no ordinary physical object. They surrounded it with the rituals

generally given kingship: one's head was to be covered in the presence of the Scroll of the Torah; hands had to be washed before touching it; one kissed the robe of this Book, just as subjects kissed the ring or robe of king or pope. These rituals were marks of respect, awe, and reverence; they were emphatically not the fearful obeisance given possessors of black magic.

This Book, and the religion of the Jews derived from it, was from the earliest days insistently anti-magic. While the other peoples and cultures of the world in which Judaism developed believed in and valued magic, the Hebrews rejected not only the gods of those cultures but also their magic. The Law was explicit: "There shall not be found among you . . . one who is a soothsayer, a diviner, or a sorcerer; one who consults with ghosts or familiar spirits, or one who inquires of the dead. For anyone who does such things is abhorrent to the Lord" Deut. 18:10-12. The penalty for such behavior was death.

Inevitably there were lapses. The attractions of magic were too great. Scripture records many tendencies to magic, notably those of Saul and Solomon, who did consult "diviners" and "familiar

54

spirits." Sometimes whole communities of Jews fell away to strange gods and practices. Yet the rejection of magic remained central to the Jewish notion of God. Miracles were acceptable, as they were believed to have been within the original plan of creation, but magic contradicted the Israelite belief in the exclusive and supreme power of *Adonai*; it contradicted the Jewish belief that the actions of humans cannot influence the actions of God.

The difference between miracle and magic is made explicit in the Exodus story: The Egyptian sorcerers duplicated the first two plagues, but not by the means used by Aaron and Moses. Pharaoh's men used their limited secret arts; Moses and Aaron did what God commanded. God suspended natural law to effect the miracles; the magicians could not.

Something more than a commandment written in Scripture was necessary in that age of magic to keep the Jews from following other gods. They were promised their own kind of beyond-human help: Legitimate prophets of the Lord would provide all the help that magicians could furnish, and more Deut. 18:15. Still, sorcery remained a constant attraction and danger, particularly in periods when it seemed that God had forgotten the Jews, as when they were conquered and carried off by the mighty, magic-following Babylonians. The prophet of that exile, Ezekiel, had to keep reminding the Jews that magic was against God's ordinances: ". . . Therefore, you shall no more see vanity, nor divine divinations . . ." Ezek. 13:23.

Saul, Solomon, and others dealt with magicians and soothsayers, and these dealings were recorded in the Bible—the Book which, the Rabbis warned, contained no magic and was not in itself magical. However, many Jews were unconvinced because they believed that the Name of God could bring death and create life in a lump of clay such as a golem. Certainly the Torah in which the Name and Word of God were revealed must have special powers, they argued.

And so it was that in medieval times, when the world around the Jews was awash in superstition, the Torah became key in a lapse into a Jewish magic. When a woman was in active labor, a Torah scroll was placed on her belly to ease the child's exit. Many rabbis railed against this practice, but seldom successfully in that age of magic. The most they could do was accept a compromise: They permitted the Scroll of the Law to be brought to the doorway of the labor room so that "the merit of the Torah may protect her."

The magic of the Book even extended to excerpts from it. The Torah enjoins us to "write them [the Words of God] upon the doorposts of your house and upon your gates" Deut. 6:9. This is done by enclosing certain passages of Torah in a case, popularly called a *mezuzah* [the Hebrew word for "doorpost"], and affixing the enclosed words to the doorpost. In medieval times the *mezuzah* was assumed to have magical powers to keep demons away; even today a *mezuzah* is viewed by some as a lucky talisman.

Even the most superstitious and unlearned Jew knew that the Book's power was not in the animal skins of which it was made, nor the ink with which it was written. The Book's power, its holiness, was in its words; words formed by its Hebrew letters. It was out of those letters—the *Midrash* refers to them as black fire written on white fire—that God fashioned the Torah.

The letters of the Hebrew alphabet have enormous power. The Torah itself came into being before creation; the letters came into being even before the Torah. They are so powerful that, as Rabbi Chezkiah says, ". . . The covenant upon which the world rests . . . is symbolized by the small letter *Yud*, the root and foundation of the world." That's just the very smallest letter! The letter *bet*, too, has power: The Sabbath was created by inserting *bet* between *shin* and *tav*. Not only the word "Sabbath" but the day itself, the day on which all the world—humans and animals, trees and insects—rests and acknowledges God.

If letters and the words they form are so powerful, the ability to manipulate these letters must confer power upon the manipulator. This idea, in combination with another persistent primitive notion, the secret name, gave rise to a powerful system of magic. The notion believed by most early cultures was that all living creatures have a secret name, and if you can discover that name you can get control over the person or thing so named.

The manipulation of letters and names was made easy by a linguistic characteristic common in ancient languages (Hebrew, Greek, Latin, etc.): letters also function as numbers.

The practice of magically manipulating letters and numbers was not invented by the Jews. We know that the Assyrian conqueror Sargon II (eighth century B.C.E.) ordered a wall to be built around his city that was to be exactly 16,283 cubits long (about five miles). Why 16,283? Because the letters that spell "Sargon" also make up the number 16,283. The Jews also used this magical art before the Common Era, and the Talmud reports that Yochanan ben Zakkai (first century C.E.) was accomplished in figuring "the heavenly revolutions and *gematria*" Baba Batra 134a.

Gematria is the term used in Jewish mysticism for the manipulation of letters-numbers. The "Baraita of 32 Rules," cited in the Talmud, recognizes several forms of *gematria* as acceptable methods of interpreting Scripture. Specifically cited are the methods called (numerical) *gematria*, *atbash*, *temurah*, and *notarikon*.

The Hebrew numbering system, which makes *gematria* possible, is a simple substitution of number for letter. The first letter, *alef*, is 1; the second letter, *bet*, is 2; the third letter, *gimmel*, is 3; and so on to the ninth letter, *tet*. The next nine let-

ters, from *yud* to *tsadee*, represent the tens—10, 20, 30, etc. The remaining four letters, *koof* to *tav*, are hundreds—100 to 400. (In some Hebrew numbering systems, the five final letter forms are used for the hundreds from 500 to 900.) All other numbers are created by combinations, as in Arabic numbers: eleven is 10 (*yud*) and 1 (*alef*); 900 is *tav* (400), *tav* (400), and *koof* (100). There are a few exceptions: The regular formation of 15 would be *yud* (10) plus *hay* (5), and 16 would be *yud* (10) plus *vav* (6). But these combinations form abbreviations of the Tetragrammaton, which is impermissible. So 15 is *tet* (9) and *vav* (6), and 16 is *tet* (9) and *zayin* (7).

Gematria opened Scripture to all kinds of new meanings. For example, the verse "When Abram heard that his brother had been taken captive, he went forth with 318 trained men . . . and pursued them . . ." Gen. 14:14. Not really, said the Rabbis. When Abram went to release Lot he didn't need an army; his servant Eliezer was enough. The number 318 spells Eliezer.

Playing with letter-number combinations was not limited to Jewish mystics, nor even to Jews generally. Moslems and Christians used gematria for both secular and religious purposes—even for anti-Jewish polemics and to prove the authenticity of their religious claims! One Arab scholar showed that Muhammed's heavenly mission was foretold in the verse "And he [Ishmael, from whom the Arabs descended] dwelt in the wilderness of Paran" Gen. 21:21. Gematria proved that Mecca and Paran are equivalent. In the verse, " . . . and I will multiply thee exceedingly," the last two words, "thee exceedingly" form the numerical equivalent of Muhammed.

The *Zohar*, a product of the Spanish Kabbalah, mentions *gematria* only in passing, but the German Kabbalists developed letter-number manipulation to a fine art. They used *gematria* to find hidden meanings in their prayers. By meditating on these esoteric meanings while in prayer, their souls were released to mount the spiritual ladder. Later, the Safed Kabbalists combined and refined all the different strands of *gematria*.

In his books, the Lurianic master Moses Cordovero listed nine systems of numerical *gematria*, among them:

1. *Simple substitution of number for letter. By this number-letter substitution, the Tetragrammaton equals 26 [10 + 5 + 6 + 5].*
2. *Simple substitution, except that for numbers above 9 only the last integer is used. The Tetragrammaton becomes 17, which equals tov, good.*
3. *Squaring the number so that bet, 2, becomes 4; gimmel, 3, becomes 9. The Tetragrammaton equals 186.*
4. *Adding the value of all preceding numbers; e.g., dalet, the fourth letter equals 1 + 2 + 3 + 4 or 10. In this system, the Tetragrammaton is 106.*
5. *Using the word as a single number, so that the Tetragrammaton comes out 10,565.*

There are many more systems, limited only by the ingenuity of the compilers, and there were at least as many systems of letter-letter substitutions as letter-number combinations. The major ones:

1. Atbash—*Substituting the last letter of the Hebrew alphabet tav, for the first, alef; the next to the last, shin, for the second letter, bet, etc.*
2. Temurah—*Various forms of "folding" the 22-letter alphabet. Fold it in half, and the 12th letter, lamed, becomes alef; the 13th letter becomes bet, etc.*
3. Atbah—*Kinds of acrostics in which the first letters, or the last letters of lines of Scripture spell out words. For instance, a powerful incantation against being hit with a deadly weapon is a word made up of the last letters of "Who is like unto You, O Lord, among the mighty"* Exod. 15:11.

4. Notarikon *[from the Latin notaricum, the name for the scribe who took shorthand notes in Roman courts]—In this system each letter of a word becomes a word beginning with that letter. This method is described in the Talmud with this illustration of the hidden meaning of the first word of the Ten Commandments:* An(o)chi. *The letters become the words* anah, nafshi, ketivah, yahavit, *or "I Myself wrote [and gave them] the Writings"* Shabbat 105a.

In another notarikon system, words are divided to form new words: the name Reuven (Reuben) *becomes* ru *and* ben: *see [the] son.*

There is a *midrash:* "The Holy One, blessed be He, said: I request laborers. The Torah told Him: I put at Your disposal 22 laborers, namely, the 22 letters of the [alphabet that formed the] Torah, and give to each his own." The tradition of *gematria* can be read in this *midrash:* Not to gain power, not to turn dross into gold, but to find the inner meanings of the words that God formed out of the letters of fire. For, as the *midrash* says, each letter is given its own meaning, task, and piece of creation.

STUDY QUESTIONS

1 According to the text, what happened when Adam sinned in the Garden of Eden? When and how was the damage repaired? What is the significance of the name Seth (the son of Adam and Eve)?

2 Explain the difference between miracle and magic.

3 Describe *gematria*. Why were masters of *gematria* given great respect and considered to be among the great mystics?

Freedom

Zohar II, 39b

"SEVEN DAYS SHALL YOU eat unleavened bread, on the very first day you shall remove leaven from your homes . . ." Exod. 12:15.

Rabbi Simeon interpreted this verse: leaven, risen bread, yeast [*seor*, *chamets*, *machmetset*] . . . all mean the same thing. They are symbols of the powers which represent pagan enemies of Israel. These powers are termed variously "evil imagination," "strange gods," "foreign domination," and "other gods." [At the first Passover] God said to Israel: All these years you have been subject to an alien power, but now you are free and shall put away leaven.

Said Rabbi Judah: If this is so, why is leaven prohibited for only these seven days?

Rabbi Simeon answered: This ceremony [of putting away the leaven] is necessary only when the Israelites demonstrate the fact of their freedom. If a king raises a man to high office, the man will celebrate his elevation for a few days, rejoicing and putting on festive clothing. After that, he celebrates only on the anniversary of his elevation.

The same is true of Israel, which also have each year a season of joy and gladness when they celebrate the high honor that the Holy One, blessed be He, bestowed when He brought them out of the power of impurity [Egyptian slavery] into the invincible power of His holiness [freedom].

"IT IS TO ME THAT the Israelites are servants; they are My servants, whom I freed from the land of Egypt. I am the Lord your God" Lev. 25:55.

According to the Rabbis, this is the central Scriptural statement on freedom. The repetition of "they are My servants" is read to mean "you are My servants, not the servants of My servants." That is, humans are the servants solely of the Lord; it is contrary to God's intention for them to be slaves of other humans.

The Law says that if a Jew voluntarily accepts slavery (or refuses freedom), a hole is pierced in his ear lobe. Why the ear lobe? Because, said Rabbi Yochanan ben Zakkai, it was with the ear that Israel heard God's statement. "It is to Me that the Israelites are servants . . ." "God can be served only by free moral agents, not by slaves" Kiddushin 22b.

The freedom cited in Scripture and by the Rabbis is freedom to worship God. For a Jew, freedom to worship God im-

58

plies physical, intellectual, and political freedom as well. Since free people cannot be compelled to serve God, not even by heaven, free will is a necessary attribute of humanity. *Yes Guido & Gigi, Tato.*

There was even a debate over whether the employee-employer relationship inhibits personal freedom. The Rabbis decided that the master-servant relationship does not inhibit freedom if the worker has the uncontested right to withdraw his labor from the master whenever he wishes.

In text after text, we are reminded of the centrality of freedom and free will:

Everything is foreseen, but freedom of choice is granted [Avot 3:19].

It can be proven by the Torah, the Prophets, and the other sacred writings, that man is led along the path which he wishes to follow [Makkot 10b].

Rabbi Chanina ben Chama said: Everything is in the power of heaven except the fear of heaven. God in His Providence determines beforehand what a man shall be and what shall befall him, but not whether he shall be righteous or wicked [Niddah 16b].

Rabbi Abba said: God deliberated how to create man. He said to Himself: If I create him like the angels, he will be immortal. If I create him like the beasts, he will be mortal. God decided to leave man's conduct to his own free choice, and if he [man] had not sinned, he would have been immortal [Genesis Rabbah 8:11].

When the Law came into the world, freedom came into the world [Genesis Rabbah 53:7].

It says: "And the tablets were the work of God, and the writing was the writing of God, graven upon the tablets" Exod. 32:16. Do not read the word *charut* [graven], but *cherut* [freedom], for no man is free but he who labors in the Torah [Avot 6:2].

Before the soul is given residence in the body of an infant about to be born, the kernel of the body is brought to the Heavenly Tribunal, where its fate is decided: whether it will be rich or poor; whether it be male or female, heroic or cowardly, tall or short, handsome or homely, fat or thin, respected or ignored. One thing, however, is not subject to predestination, namely whether the child will be good or bad, since it must have freedom of will [*Tanchuma* to Leviticus (*Tazria*)].

7:57 P.M.
Nov. 11/08

STUDY QUESTIONS

1 What is the mystical interpretation of the Passover custom of *bedikat chamets* (putting away the leaven)?

2 Discuss the meaning of the verse from Makkot: "It can be proven by the Torah, the Prophets, and the other sacred writings, that man is led along the path which he wishes to follow." How does this verse relate to the necessity of human freedom?

3 "If a king raises a man to high office, the man will celebrate his elevation for a few days, rejoicing and putting on festive clothing. After that, he celebrates only on the anniversary of his elevation." What is the hidden meaning of this quotation from *Zohar*?

4 As this course of study draws to a close, can you summarize the main aspects of belief in Kabbalah? What draws you personally toward such belief? Are there any elements of this belief which remain foreign, or even obnoxious to you? Has studying Jewish mysticism changed your opinions about Kabbalah and the *Zohar* in any important ways?

Mary Swana – "Boys in the Trees"

                        that
"The only thing you cannot escape from is yourself."

            Joseph Boyden